# THERAPEUTIC APPF
# WITH BABIES AND YOUNG
# CHILDREN IN CARE

*Therapeutic Approaches for Babies and Young Children in Care: Observation and Attention* is about the value of observation and close attention for babies and young children who may be vulnerable to psychological and attachment difficulties. Case studies explore the potential for observation-based therapeutic approaches to support caregivers, social workers, and professional networks. A third theme in the book is the roots of observation-based approaches in psychoanalytic infant observation and the contribution of these ways of working to professional training and continuing development.

Using case examples, Jenifer Wakelyn illustrates observational ways of working that can be practised by professionals and family members to help children express themselves and feel understood. The interventions focus on the early stages of life in care and on the "golden thread" of relationships with caregivers. The book explores contemporary neuroscience and child development research alongside psychoanalytic theory to illustrate the role of attention in helping children to develop the internal continuity that sustains the personality and protects against the fragmenting impact of trauma.

*Therapeutic Approaches for Babies and Young Children in Care* is written for social workers, teachers, medical staff, and other professionals whose work brings them in contact with the youngest children in care; it will also be relevant for commissioners, managers, and trainers as well as mental health clinicians who are starting to work with children in care. It will provide a valuable insight into the lives of infants and young children in the care system and the applications of psychoanalytic infant observation.

**Jenifer Wakelyn** is a Child and Adolescent Psychotherapist at the Tavistock and Portman NHS Foundation Trust. She works in a mental health service for children in care and teaches and supervises in the clinical training in child psychotherapy at the Tavistock Centre. She has presented research on therapeutic intervention with babies and young children in care across the UK and in Europe and the Ukraine.

# Tavistock Clinic Series

Margot Waddell, Jocelyn Catty, & Kate Stratton (Series Editors)

## Recent titles in the Tavistock Clinic Series

# THERAPEUTIC APPROACHES WITH BABIES AND YOUNG CHILDREN IN CARE

## Observation and Attention

*Jenifer Wakelyn*

Foreword by
*Dilys Daws*

Routledge
Taylor & Francis Group

LONDON AND NEW YORK

First published 2020
by Routledge
2 Park Square, Milton Park, Abingdon, Oxon OX14 4RN

and by Routledge
52 Vanderbilt Avenue, New York, NY 10017

*Routledge is an imprint of the Taylor & Francis Group, an informa business*

*British Library Cataloguing-in-Publication Data*
A catalogue record for this book is available from the British Library

*Library of Congress Cataloging-in-Publication Data*
A catalog record has been requested for this book

ISBN: 978-0-367-25136-9 (hbk)
ISBN: 978-1-78220-438-1 (pbk)
ISBN: 978-0-429-28627-8 (ebk)

Typeset in Palatino
by Swales & Willis, Exeter, Devon, UK
Printed and bound by CPI Group (UK) Ltd, Croydon CR0 4YY

*In memory of my mother*

# CONTENTS

*Margot Waddell, Jocelyn Catty, & Kate Stratton*

Since it was founded in 1920, the Tavistock Clinic—now the Tavistock and Portman NHS Foundation Trust—has developed a wide range of developmental approaches to mental health which have been strongly influenced by the ideas of psychoanalysis. It has also adopted systemic family therapy as a theoretical model and a clinical approach to family problems. The Tavistock is now one of the largest mental health training institutions in Britain. It teaches up to 600 students a year on postgraduate, doctoral, and qualifying courses in social work, systemic psychotherapy, psychology, psychiatry, nursing, and child, adolescent, and adult psychotherapy, along with 2,000 multidisciplinary clinicians, social workers, and teachers attending Continuing Professional Development courses and conferences on psychoanalytic observation, psychoanalytic thinking, and management and leadership in a range of clinical and community settings.

The Tavistock's philosophy aims at promoting therapeutic methods in mental health. Its work is based on the clinical expertise that is also the basis of its consultancy and research activities. The aim of this Series is to make available to the reading public the clinical, theoretical, and research work that is most influential at the Tavistock. The Series sets out new approaches in the understanding and treatment of psychological disturbance in children, adolescents, and adults, both as individuals and in families.

Jenifer Wakelyn's description of *Therapeutic Approaches with Babies and Young Children in Care* underlines how closely the book fits with the philosophy of the Tavistock and the Series:"[This] work in progress …is informed by clinical practice and research, but above all by encounters with children and the adults looking after them and working to support them." Her thoughtful and moving book places at the centre of its gaze both the children who cannot grow up in their families of origin and the adults who take on their care. The book is framed by an Introduction that brings alive the universality of fostering and adoption and an Afterword that focuses on "attention" and its "fundamental role in allowing a child to feel held in mind and to develop over time the internal continuity that sustains the personality".

The therapeutic and research work described in these pages is based on the fundamental principles of infant observation that underpin the training of psychoanalytic child and adolescent psychotherapists, but are here developed into two forms. First, Wakelyn describes the therapeutic observation that was also the subject of her doctoral research, and its applications in a specialist mental health service. Later, she describes the therapeutic approach "Watch Me Play!"—named by the five-year-old son of a friend—which distils these principles into a powerful therapeutic tool for foster carers.

This book treads lightly over the trauma—of broken attachments and worse—of children and infants who cannot be looked after in their birth families. While never shying from its impact, Wakelyn chooses to show how the traumatized child may be helped to grow and flourish. As she says, she could have written "a different book, about the catastrophic trajectories" that lead some children with such backgrounds through multiple failed placements into residential care and/or a range of adverse outcomes. She opts, instead, to bear witness to "children's receptivity to adult attention, their eloquence if someone is watching and listening". The vignettes and close descriptions she uses to bring this alive are indeed compelling. As she concludes: "Whereas the dynamics of trauma are dominated by the compulsion to repeat, a group that is gathered together by attention has the potential to give birth to something new and lively."

Wakelyn's allusion to the "group" in relation to the child encompasses both the foster carer and his or her family, the social worker, and the wider professional network. Indeed, *Therapeutic Approaches with Babies and Young Children in Care* attests to the collaborative process, the importance of a joined-up approach to support both the carer and the cared-for, and includes a chapter co-written with her colleagues Marta Bacigalupi and Martina Weilandt. Between them, the authors draw upon psychoanalytic child psychotherapy, clinical psychology, social work, and primary mental health care; the depth and sensitivity shown in the work and case studies described express, in a clear and accessible style, what has been learned from long and often painful experience. As Dilys Daws writes in her eloquent Foreword, reading *Therapeutic Approaches for Babies and Young Children in Care* will be "therapeutic for many professionals who may feel daunted and overwhelmed by trying to help children whose lives have been severely disrupted and who have lost trust that they will ever be genuinely 'seen'."

# ACKNOWLEDGEMENTS

I would like to thank many people who have helped me in writing this book.

I am indebted to my teachers, supervisors, and colleagues at the Tavistock. Dilys Daws and Roberta Mondadori were my first observation tutors, and I also thank Dilys for her Foreword. I wish to thank Deborah Steiner. I am grateful to my colleagues in First Step and in the local authority for our work together; to William Halton for his help and guidance; and to Wendy Lobatto for her consistent support for clinical research and work with young children in care.

I owe special thanks to Tatjana, Thorsten, and Elias, and to Sam.

I thank the members of the Tavistock Fostering and Adoption workshop and participants in the Watch Me Play! evaluation project for their feedback and contributions to discussions. Friends and colleagues have given me support, criticism, advice, and suggestions; I particularly thank Claudia Carr, Marta Cioeta, Kathryn Fenton, Patrizia Gatti, Ruth Gilbert, Julia Gannon, Jackie Hall, Carol Hardy, Jonathan Hill, Thomas Hillen, Jeanne Kaniuk, Eilis Kennedy, Jenny Kenrick, Anoushka Khan, Kasia Macholla, Eamon McCrory, Elizabeth Meins, Sheila Miller, Elizabeth Murphy, Alice Noon, Giuseppe Paladino, Tatjana Pushkaryova, Mike Shaw, John Simmonds, Maria Rhode, Margaret and Michael Rustin, Brenda and Leah Taylor, Luisa Carbone Tirelli, Judith Trowell, Carlos Vasquez, and Gianna Williams.

I gratefully acknowledge funding from the Tavistock Clinic Foundation and a sabbatical from the Tavistock Child and Family Directorate which made research on Watch Me Play! possible. I thank the Foundling Museum, London, and Bridgeman Images for permission to reproduce Hogarth's *Moses Brought before Pharaoh's Daughter*.

Jocelyn Catty, Sarah Colquhoun, Imogen Davies, Dilys Daws, Anna Fitzgerald, Jane Hunter, Naomi Misonoo, and Martina Weilandt kindly read the text and made many useful comments and suggestions. I thank Martina Weilandt and Marta Bacigalupi for their contributions to chapter 5. I am grateful to the Tavistock Clinic Series editors, Margot Waddell, Jocelyn Catty, and Kate Stratton, for their consistent support and constructive advice, and to Charles Bath, the Routledge editor, for his calm oversight of the publication process.

I thank my husband, David Matthews, who made helpful comments on the text and has given me confidence and encouragement at every stage.

Above all, I am grateful to the children, families, and professionals I have learned from.

# FOREWORD

## Dilys Daws

This is an inspiring book. It has an unusual basis: Jenifer Wakelyn's early interest in the history of art, in the beauty and emotional depth in many historical paintings, imbues the book. Jenifer learned to "see" these paintings, and she brings the close attention, the patience, the emotional intensity, and the discovery of meaning into her work as a child and adolescent psychotherapist, especially using ideas from psychoanalytic observation. The beautiful painting of a child on the cover of the book is a clue to the depth of the feelings and ideas expressed in the book. Jenifer pays attention to the situation of babies and children taken into care. The title of one kind of approach, "Watch Me Play!", comes from not just seeing, but listening to one child and recognizing the child's creativity.

Jenifer and I first met when she came to my infant observation seminars 22 years ago at the start of her training as a child psychotherapist. At the time, we could still offer these seminars at home, adding an extra dimension of a personal setting to the work. I like to think that my sitting-room, lined with paintings, some by my first husband, an Australian artist, enriched the seminars and perhaps made a link between Jenifer and myself.

Keeping to the theme of the paintings, Hogarth's painting of Moses vividly illustrates "the breaking of the continuity of the line of the individual's existence" that Winnicott describes as the essence of trauma.

This is one of the main themes of the book. As Jenifer says, it depicts "a child on the brink of a move away from his familiar world, confronting a step he must take alone".

Much of the book is heart-breaking. While I was reading it, a friend told me that her adult son fondly remembered his childhood Christmas presents: "You knew exactly what stage of development we were at and what we would love to play with." This book is about the consequences for a child of not being known intimately, but it is also optimistic. It supports the adults involved with the child—foster carers, adoptive parents, and professionals—all in themselves having to bear the knowledge of the deprivation these children have endured. Jenifer offers the hope that understanding the child now can help repair some of the damage. As she says: "The observational ways of working that are illustrated aim to help children feel that their experiences can be understood and thought about by others. They also aim to help caregivers to connect with children who may have lost, or never had, trust in adults to look after them."

The experience of reading this book will be therapeutic for many professionals who may feel daunted and overwhelmed by trying to help children whose lives have been severely disrupted and who have lost trust that they will ever be genuinely "seen". Jenifer's calm, insightful, but very knowledgeable style makes one trust in her. She is also generous and quotes many child psychotherapy colleagues from the Tavistock whose own writings also show how the application of psychoanalytic ideas and especially of psychoanalytic observation are able to help the wider fields of social work and mental health.

Jenifer shows courage in recognizing and writing about the many difficulties that face children in care. To end, it is worth highlighting one of the most positive points that she makes: that "overall, children's views about fostering are remarkably positive". For some children, foster care brings the first experience of "having a proper family who care about me".

# Introduction

Throughout the ages, in every culture, foster carers and adoptive parents have provided love and nurture for children who cannot be looked after in their birth families. With the stability and love of a new family, many children thrive; but for some children, adversity continues. Trauma, deprivation, and care from multiple caregivers can all impact on the capacity of adults to respond to the psychological needs of vulnerable infants and young children. Emotional difficulties may be less at the forefront of adult attention when there have been anxieties about keeping the child safe or deciding who is the right person to look after the child. Knowledge about important events and relationships may be lost if many different adults are involved in the child's care; a child who is moved to the care of unfamiliar adults, or who is not confident that adults can be trusted, may be left with memories and experiences that he or she cannot communicate yet cannot manage alone.

This book is about therapeutic approaches that aim to support babies and young children in care and their caregivers. It sets out to explore the scope for caregivers and professionals in the care system to mitigate the impact of discontinuities for infants and young children living beyond the "family envelope". Written primarily for social workers, teachers, medical staff, and other professionals whose work brings them in contact with the youngest children in care, it may also be relevant for commissioners and managers. I hope, too, that it may be relevant for mental health clinicians interested in the wider contexts of children in care, and in the applications of psychoanalytic infant observation, and for the general reader with an interest in understanding more about how infants and young children come to be in the care system and what may happen to them.

The work in progress described in this book is informed by clinical practice and research but, above all, by encounters with children and the adults looking after them and working to support them. The observational ways of working that are illustrated aim to help children to feel that their experiences can be understood and thought about by others. They also aim to help caregivers to connect with children who may have lost, or never had, trust in adults to look after them. Two types of approach are described: therapeutic observation, a specialist, medium- to long-term clinical approach for children with complex difficulties or in troubled circumstances; and Watch Me Play!, a briefer approach that can be used by professionals and family members alike. Watch Me Play! can be put into place rapidly and can contribute to a better understanding of a child's strengths and interests as well as of any worries or difficulties.

## Children in transition

In 2016–2017, almost 13,000 babies and young children aged between birth and four years were taken into care, over a third of all children who enter care in England each year. All children in care have crossed a basic divide from parents to substitute caregivers, and they have experienced the breaking of "the family envelope" (Houzel, 1996). For some children, their development may have been compromised by foetal exposure to drugs or alcohol, or by the traumas of abuse and neglect. Defensive adaptations to early trauma and to disrupted relationships with primary caregivers may then compound these early difficulties in life.

The effects of early difficulty in the parent–child or caregiver–child relationship are universally recognized as significant and long-lasting. Yet repeated policy calls for greater investment in early intervention have had little or no impact on funding, even though the potential benefits of early intervention have been clearly demonstrated by health care economists (Allen, 2011; APPG, 2015). A significant increase in the number of children in care in the UK—72,670 in 2016–2017, compared to 59,500 in 2008–2009 (DfE, 2017)—seems to reflect among other factors the impact of cuts to children's centres and to early help and support services for parents since the financial crisis of 2008 (Family Rights Group, 2018). Social changes and cultural trends that are less favourable to sensitive parenting may also have contributed to the increase in the number of children who cannot be looked after by their families.

Moving to new caregivers is a central experience shared by all children who cannot be looked after by their parents. In another age, the same dynamics appear: Hogarth's painting of Moses as a young child, on display today in London's Foundling Museum, takes us to the heart of the transitions experienced, sometimes repeatedly, by children in the care system. In the bible story, having placed her baby in a basket where he could be found by the daughter of the Egyptian ruler, to save him from a decree that all male new-born babies would be killed, the mother of Moses presented herself as a wet-nurse who could take care of the infant.

*Figure 1 Moses Brought before Pharaoh's Daughter* (1746), by William Hogarth [1697–1764]. (Coram in the care of the Foundling Museum, London/ Bridgeman Images.)

Established by Thomas Coram in 1739, in its first four years the Foundling Hospital took in almost 15,000 orphans and babies given up by mothers who could not look after them. Hogarth and his wife were early supporters, and they fostered several babies before they were taken to live at the Hospital at the age of four or five years (Uglow, 1997). His painting vividly illustrates the "breaking of the continuity of the line of the individual's existence" that the twentieth-century paediatrician and psychoanalyst Donald Winnicott describes as the essence of trauma (1967, p. 22). The painting has an intimacy unusual in a public work. The imminent separation is poignantly conveyed through a language of the hands: the child's tense grip in the shadows of his mother's robe contrasting with the brightly lit, outstretched hand of the reclining princess. Hogarth seems to have brought his experiences of separations to bear in his portrayal of a child on the brink of a move away from his familiar world, confronting a step that he must take alone.

## Outline of the book

The first chapter offers a selective review of classic and recent research on adversities affecting babies and young children in care, drawing on the extensive research literatures on infant mental health, maltreatment, and substitute care. The chapter outlines the benefits that foster care can bring for abused and neglected children and explores factors that can either impede or promote the loving and attentive nurture that every child needs. Chapter 2 describes the model of psychoanalytic infant observation first developed at the Tavistock Clinic in the 1940s and now widely used in mental health and social care trainings across the world. This chapter goes on to explore therapeutic ways of working with vulnerable children based on close observation that aim to bring a focus on psychological experience and the primacy of relationships.

Some readers may prefer to start with chapters 3 and 4, which present and discuss a ten-month therapeutic observation of a baby in his foster home, which I carried out as clinical research. Chapter 5, which has been written together with my colleagues Marta Bacigalupi and Martina Weilandt, gives examples of therapeutic observation applied in a specialist mental health service. Chapter 6 describes and illustrates the development of a brief intervention, Watch Me Play!, and the final chapter (chapter 7) gives an overview of practice considerations for this approach. Much of the material in chapter 7 comes from discussions with social workers, foster carers, adoptive parents, contact supervisors, and health professionals as part of a project funded by the

Tavistock Clinic Foundation. For reasons of confidentiality, participants are not named, but I am grateful for all of their contributions. The Afterword offers concluding reflections on the nature of attention and the significance of observation for psychological growth and well-being.

All of the case histories have been disguised to protect confidentiality. Some of the shorter clinical vignettes are composite examples, but all are derived from work in specialist mental health services with children in care. The circumstances leading to children coming into care, and the difficulties and distress that some children continue to face, are harrowing. I hope that the clinical examples, while they may stir up much in the reader, also illustrate the children's eloquence and zest for development and the commitment of their caregivers and supporting professionals.

## A note on terminology

"Children in care" and "looked-after children" have become more or less synonymous terms in the UK. I mainly use the former.

# CHAPTER ONE

# Being seen

Interaction with a responsive adult is intimately connected with a baby's development from the first moments of life. As parents think about their baby and try to understand what he or she might be feeling, they are providing something very important for their baby's development. When a parent is able to be attentive to a baby who is crying, powerful feelings such as fear, hunger, or discomfort can be made sense of, and the baby has the experience of being attended to and thought about. Repeated interactions of this kind allow the baby to develop the expectation of being responded to, taken seriously, cared for, and helped. The psychoanalyst Wilfred Bion (1962) called this emotional linking between baby and parent "containment". For Winnicott, the receptivity and responsiveness to the baby's moods and needs that a mother intuitively provides is a form of "holding" that allows the baby to have a feeling of "going-on-being" (1962). A parent's heightened preoccupation with the baby's needs seems to be nature's way of reinforcing the parent–child bond.

Containment provides the basis for emotional growth: the infant's raw and powerful feelings are taken in, while also a change is brought about in them. When the feelings are understood, put into words, or simply accepted by the caregiving adult, they become more digestible, less overwhelming. The child psychotherapist Shirley Hoxter puts it like this:

The mother who is not too immersed in her own difficulties replies to the infant's behaviour, his varied cries, his kicks and screams, his inertia or limpness, his smiles and gurgles, as though she believes that such behaviour is a meaningful communication which requires to be understood and responded to. Her response is probably an essential prerequisite enabling the baby gradually to build up some form of realization of his own that behaviour is meaningful and communicative. Such experience accumulates from innumerable little incidents. [1977, p. 215]

Psychoanalytic writers and child development researchers who come to the study of childhood from different perspectives agree that the earliest experiences with caregivers are formative. The Harvard Center for the Developing Child (2018) uses the metaphor of "serve and return" to describe cycles of attuned interaction between child and caregiver. The baby "serves", sending a signal as he slightly opens his mouth, moves his tongue, or lifts his eyebrows. The parent or caregiver, watching closely, "returns" by echoing the infant's facial expression, perhaps slightly amplifying it, introducing a slight variation, or accompanying the return signal with a matching sound. The infant watches the face of the adult with equally rapt attention, and further sequences of "serve and return" bring a glow to the face of baby and adult alike, until the baby turns away for a rest. During these interactive sequences, pleasurable hormones are released that motivate baby and parent to come back for more, reinforcing the bond between child and caregiver (Ungar, 2017).

[A]n enormous amount of the activity of the child during the first year and a half of life is extraordinarily social and communicative. . . . When the child's attachment to the mother (or caretaker) is initially assured by a variety of innate response patterns, there very quickly develops a reciprocity that the infant comes to anticipate and count on. [Bruner, 1983, p. 72]

In her book, *Why Love Matters*, Sue Gerhardt (2015) provides an engrossing account of neuroscientific discoveries that have confirmed the suppositions of the first psychoanalysts about the formative nature of early experience. Another readable account is provided by Lynne Murray and Liz Andrews in their book *The Social Baby: Understanding Babies' Communication from Birth* (2005), which is illustrated with photographs.

During moments of close reciprocal attention, the infant's physiological systems are fully activated (Music, 2016). New connections being made in the infant's brain—and even, to a lesser degree, in the brain of the responding adult—promote the capacities for recognizing emotions and for thinking. A baby whose parent or caregiver attends closely to his signals experiences a range of emotions in response to the expressive face and voice of his partner in this interactive "dance". In *Finding Your Way with Your Baby: The Emotional Life of Parents and Babies* (2015), Dilys Daws and Alex de Rementeria describe how, in gaining the fundamental security of experiencing his or her feelings being understood and known by another person, the baby also comes to know about the range of human feelings. In ordinary parenting, the to and fro of responsive interaction is repeated innumerable times. Following the misunderstandings and interruptions that are part of the fabric of daily life, efforts to work out what went wrong, and to repair, help the infant–parent couple to get back on track. Being seen and attended to, and becoming re-attuned after an interruption or a mismatch, are fundamental experiences of relating to another that enable infants, over time, to come to know their own feelings (Stern, 2004; Trevarthen, 2001). Infants who regularly experience these everyday but highly complex interactions gradually develop the ability to regulate their feelings for themselves.

## Adversity in infancy

### Trauma and the response to trauma

The fundamental early experiences of being seen and responded to in safe, nurturing, and stimulating ways are interrupted, or may never have become established, for children who cannot be looked after by their parents. Babies who lack these experiences of attunement, or have significantly less of them, are more likely to struggle in their development. In the absence of an understanding or comforting response, the feelings of an infant who is totally dependent on adult caregivers intensify; if this goes on longer than the infant can bear, the feelings are likely to be experienced as overwhelmingly bad, just needing to be got rid of. Neuroscientists have discovered pathways through which the resulting "toxic stress" can become entrenched in the infant's brain (Perry, Pollard, Blakley, Baker, & Vigilante, 1995; Schore, 2001). Survival modes that protect the self from immediate danger bypass the parts of the brain that recognize and regulate emotion. When these areas of the brain fail to develop, defensive responses such as hypervigilance, dysregulation, and dissociation continue to interfere with play, social interaction, and learning long after the danger has passed.

Traumatic events remain encoded in body and mind in the form of sensory memories or flashbacks that can be instantly triggered by later stimuli. Patterns of brain activity in children who have been exposed to family violence have been found to be similar to those of soldiers exposed to combat (McCrory, De Brito, & Viding, 2011). The physiological systems for responding to threat are fully activated, while the systems in the brain that store, recognize, and respond to positive, loving, and affectionate experiences are less well developed, meaning that these aspects of experience are less available as a resource for the individual.

Mental health problems and transgenerational family difficulties are often the context in which abuse and neglect lead to children entering care. Maltreatment, in the forms of physical, sexual or emotional abuse, neglect, and severe family dysfunction are the most common reasons for children being taken into care (DfE, 2017). These adversities, cumulative in their impact, are likely to be compounded by a lack of the attuned interactions that are fundamental for early development, as parents who harm their children are more likely to have difficulty in responding to their child's cues (Brandon et al., 2014). In their report, *Missed Opportunities: Indicators of Neglect—What Is Ignored, Why, and What Can Be Done?* (2014), Marian Brandon and colleagues highlight neglect as the most common form of maltreatment, as harmful, or more harmful, in the long term than physical or sexual abuse. Children who are severely neglected grow up in chaotic conditions and squalor, with no regular routines for feeding, sleeping, or toileting; they may be exposed to accidental injury and to unknown adults. Some children receive little or no affection, attention, or stimulation. Failures of supervision that result in children being exposed to violence and conflict between adults and to unboundaried sexual activity also come under the heading of neglect.

When the basic needs for loving nurture and responsive attention remain unmet, a profound lack of self-worth and self-agency can ensue, leading to withdrawal and, in extreme situations, failure to thrive. Children can be exposed to severe neglect for years unless or until physical injuries alert professional attention. Many foster carers are profoundly shocked by the states in which neglected child come to their care. When neglect has been severe and long-standing, children may be undernourished and may steal and hoard food, while others may be grossly obese. Some toddlers and young children are unable to stand or walk, having been kept strapped into buggies for many hours of the day. Some children are startlingly indiscriminate in approaching strangers. Others withdraw and barely react to the presence of others, neither showing distress nor seeking comfort. Some children who have been deprived of loving affection engage in comfort-seeking sensory activity, which may follow exposure to adult sexuality or sexual abuse or may be a substitute for physical affection and comfort. Many neglected children have delayed speech and language, and their medical and dental needs have often not been addressed.

The ordinarily thriving baby is a magnet for adult attention, but some babies may respond to extreme stress by developing defensive ways of relating that deflect adult attention. It is harder to notice and respond to infants when their cues and signals are fleeting, muted, or shockingly different from what we expect. Studies by Selma Fraiberg and colleagues in the US recorded the reactions of babies from age three months towards their mothers who had severe mental health difficulties (1982). The babies, who received treatment together with their parents, had been so frightened by their mothers that they did not look at them or seek to be close to them. Some babies showed no sign whatsoever of recognition when looking in their mother's direction, or when their mother spoke, and seemed frozen and cut off from feeling. These babies were unable to turn to their mothers for help, and when fear, distress, or discomfort broke through the barrier of dissociation, the storm of feeling was so extreme that they could not be consoled either by their parents or by the clinicians:

> The same babies who avoid their mothers present another part of the story in states of distress. Hunger, solitude, state transitions, a sudden noise, or a stimulus that cannot even be identified can trigger states of helplessness and disorganization in these babies, together with screaming and flailing about—a frenzy that gathers momentum to a climax which ends in exhaustion. [Fraiberg, 1982, p. 619]

Fraiberg's work led to the development of an extensive programme of early interventions in the US and to the establishment of the World Association for Infant Mental Health. Esther Bick, the psychoanalyst who first introduced infant observation into child psychotherapy training in the UK, described similar survival mechanisms in early infancy which she called "second-skin" defences (1968). The idea is that when there is containment and continuity in an infant's care, the infant develops a "psychic skin", equivalent to the physical skin surrounding the body.

When containment is faulty or lacking, for whatever reason, the baby may resort to substitute, "second-skin" defences that rely on muscular tension in order to hold together parts of the self, in the absence of a psychic skin. These ways of protecting the self against primitive terrors can take the form of continuous restless movement, withdrawal inside a shell of muscular rigidity, or holding tight to something hard and solid. Bick saw the constant movement that drives some children who have been exposed to trauma as a defence against primitive fears of falling and falling apart, on the unconscious premise that "if you do not stop, you cannot fall".

Trauma and the responses that trauma sets going have the potential to significantly impact on long-term development and the capacities for self-regulation, attachment, and psychological well-being.

## Under-recognition of infant mental health needs

In a seminal review of child maltreatment in the UK published in *The Lancet*, Ruth Gilbert and colleagues (2009) emphasize that the incidence of child abuse and neglect is much higher than is commonly thought. Unconscious defences that can be elicited against awareness of the mental and physical pain of the most vulnerable children can distort the mind's capacity to function (Britton, 1983; Rustin, 2005; Steiner, 1985, 1993). The powerful emotions evoked by child maltreatment may result in the experiences of pre-verbal children being overlooked (Emanuel, 2006). A study of social work practice in child protection carried out by Harry Ferguson shows how this can happen. Practitioners who felt unsupported and isolated in intimidating situations became more likely to "defend themselves from unbearable feelings by detaching physically and emotionally and even completely dissociating from those they are seeking to help" (Ferguson, 2017, p. 1011). This study highlights that robust structures of co-working and reflective supervision are essential in order to equip child protection professionals to carry out their tasks, particularly when family members are felt to be intimidating.

Unrecognized distress can become a further aspect of adversity for babies and young children in care. When children have been injured, or are at risk of significant harm, the necessary focus on their physical safety can, inadvertently, result in the psychological dimensions of their experience becoming overlooked. The idea that infants are too young to have feelings retains a powerful hold; indeed, it seems to be re-invented in each generation. In 1982, Fraiberg alluded to pioneering research by René Spitz (1945) on the impact of trauma in infancy and claimed that, "Since 1945, it has not been possible to say that an infant does not experience love and loss and grief" (1982, p. 612). Nevertheless, over thirty years later, a study of minority ethnic children in the care system found "a prevailing view that infants do not *have* needs, other than basic physical ones" (Selwyn et al., 2008). Responses from social workers, clinicians, adoptive parents, and foster carers across the UK confirmed this finding in the study summarized in chapter 7, in which one participant commented, "They are this kind of forgotten" (cf. Wakelyn, 2018). Many participants also reported on a lack of services and a lack of attention to the psychological needs of the youngest children in care.

Under-recognition of infant mental health difficulties may be compounded by defensive patterns of interaction that lead even very young infants to shut down. Children who lack experiences of bringing joy and delight into their parents' lives may have a sense of themselves as empty and without value or identity. The sense of shame that can follow rejection and unmet need creates the impulse to hide. Busy foster homes can also create routines where children's physical needs are met but the fundamental needs for individual attention and intimacy are overlooked (Meakings & Selwyn, 2016). A study by Carol Hardy and colleagues (2013) of children who experienced severe stress showed that their withdrawal could lead to attention being deflected away from them and the ordinary response of adults to help a child in need being muted.

> Many young toddlers and 3–5-year-olds presented with behaviours that did not convey their needs or distress directly to the carer and therefore did not elicit nurturing responses . . . some children would communicate distress or frustration but then reject their carers' attempts to help or comfort them. Carers tended to feel that they should wait for the child to signal readiness for closer contact, but as avoidant responses were so clearly ingrained in many children . . . a pattern of distant relating between carer and child could become an established norm. [Hardy et al., 2013, p. 271]

## Under-referral

> Pre-school children in care constitute a high-risk group for mental health and developmental disorders. Without age-appropriate assessments, their needs go undetected, and opportunities for early intervention are being missed. [Hillen, Gafson, Drage, & Conlan, 2012, p. 411]

Studies in the UK and in the US report prevalences between 45% and 60% of mental health difficulties in children in care under the age of five years (Dimigen, Del Priore, & Butler, 1999; Klee, Kronstadt, & Zlotnick, 1997; McAuley & Young, 2006; McCann, James, Wilson, & Dunn, 1996; Meltzer, Corbin, Gatward, Goodman, & Ford, 2003; Stahmer et al., 2005; Urquiza, Wirtz, Peterson, & Singer, 1994). But infants and young children in care are rarely referred to mental health services until later in childhood, when their difficulties may be much harder to treat. The complexities of assessment and of access to services present obstacles to the recognition and treatment of infant mental health difficulty. Mental health assessment for pre-school children is complex in itself; Lieberman (2002, p. 5) considers that "the developmental plasticity of babies and toddlers is used against them to justify the absence of timely interventions". For looked-after children, further obstacles are presented by the difficulty of compiling a full medical and developmental history and the number of different services that may be involved (Reams, 1999). Fears of stigma or of being blamed and the wish to help the child without further professional involvement can also deter carers and social workers from pursuing a referral to child mental health services.

In many areas, there is no service to refer to, as infant mental health services have been decommissioned. Funding cuts coinciding with a significant increase in self-harm and suicidality among children and teenagers have led to a reduction in services for younger children: many child mental health services now do not accept referrals for those aged under five (Association of Child Psychotherapists, 2018). The resulting high and narrow thresholds for accessing child and adolescent mental health services may deter GPs and social workers from referring young children; but denial of the effects of trauma may also be a factor (Callaghan, Young, Pace, & Vostanis, 2004). Professionals may also be reluctant to refer infants and young children for psychological help, because of a lack of confidence that an intervention would help.

*Attachment patterns*

Attachment research provides another perspective on the influence of defensive responses established early in infancy. The pioneering studies by John Bowlby and Mary Ainsworth identified consistent patterns of attachment that seemed to be shaped by children's first experiences of caregivers (Ainsworth, Blehar, Waters, & Wall, 1978; Bowlby, 1969; see also Howe, 2005; Prior & Glaser, 2006). In the experimental situation they devised, the "Strange Situation Test", a child plays with toys in the company of his or her mother. The mother leaves the room, and a stranger enters; a few minutes later, the mother returns and greets the child.

Surprisingly consistent patterns in children's responses to their returning parent became apparent. Some children protest and show anxiety when left with the stranger; they seek comfort and closeness from the mother when she returns; reassured and comforted, they are then able to return to play. This attachment pattern is described as "secure." Children whose attachment pattern is described as "insecure" do not turn to the returning parent for comfort or reassurance. They may appear unaffected, showing neither distress at the separation nor relief at the reunion. Children with this insecure attachment pattern give every appearance of being self-sufficient but, underneath their surface calmness, high levels of tension are experienced in the form of stress hormones, muscular rigidity, and increased heart rate. Insecurely attached children learn early on not to give clear signals when they are distressed and not to seek comfort from their primary caregiver. This attachment pattern is associated with increased risk of mental health difficulties, such as anxiety and depression, in later childhood and in adult life.

Children who have been severely abused are more likely to respond to separation and reunion with their caregiver in ways that are less coherent. This group of children have no predictable way of responding to their caregiver. Their responses to the returning parent are bizarre and sometimes distressing to observe: they may freeze or bang their heads. They may rush towards, then veer away from, their parent. These children, who are likely to have experienced their parents or caregivers as frightening or frightened, have an attachment pattern that is described as "disorganized". Disorganized attachment can result from physical, emotional, or sexual abuse, or from more subtle conflictual messages that children cannot process. Their parents, who may themselves struggle with unresolved traumas, tend to behave in unpredictable ways that leave the child feeling "fear without solution" (Main & Solomon, 1980). Disorganized attachment is strongly associated with severe mental health difficulties in childhood and in adult life.

> [D]ysfunctional parental responses actually disturb the body's natural rhythms. Normally, being aroused physiologically by some intense emotional state will lead to action of some kind, and then once the feeling has been expressed, the organism will wind down and come back to a resting state. . . . But if arousal isn't soothed, this rhythm can be disrupted. . . . The cardiovascular system, in particular, will remain activated even if feelings are suppressed. . . . There is then turbulence within the system rather than straightforward processing of emotional states. [Gerhardt, 2015, p. 43]

Avoidant and disorganized attachment patterns can lead even very young children to reject comfort from caregivers. Children whose attachment patterns are insecure or disorganized may be experienced by those around them as "controlling" or "manipulative" because of their sudden and sometimes alarming mood swings. At the other extreme, lethargy or withdrawal can be mistaken for contentment. As Fraiberg saw with the distressed infants she was treating, when unrelieved distress becomes intolerable, it breaks through in ways that can seem unpredictable or disproportionate. The comfort offered by a parent or a substitute caregiver may be rejected by a child who seems to dismiss any show of feeling, leaving adults who try to reach out to the child feeling discouraged and more likely, in turn, to withdraw from the child.

> [E]ngaging in a positive, warm, consistent and constructive way with children who have experienced maltreatment can be challenging to their carers. If a child is hypervigilant to threat, less sensitive to reward, and has fewer emotion regulation and executive functioning skills, they can often evoke negative feelings and a sense of inadequacy in those who are trying to meet their needs. [Gerin, Hanson, Viding, & McCrory, 2019]

It is important to address defensive ways of relating as early as possible so that the psychological needs for intimacy and trust, but also for exploration and individuation, can be met. Although both attachment and exploration are integral to attachment theory, exploration has received far less attention in research and in professional trainings. Bowlby (1969) described attachment and exploration as two interacting systems, both needed for development.

> The attachment system exists to bring the infant into close proximity with its caregiver, thereby protecting the infant from harm and predation. The exploration system exists to propel the infant into the world to learn about the environment, thereby enhancing the likelihood of its safe and effective functioning. [Elliot & Reis, 2003, p. 320]

Attachment difficulties can be mitigated by later reparative relationships (Rutter, 1998, 2003), but children for whom this does not happen may experience a double impairment. When attachment needs are satisfied, a child can explore, taking an interest in the world beyond the parent, in new relationships and in play. When attachment needs remain unsatisfied, exploration is inhibited and the capacity to embrace new interests and experiences is circumscribed. A child who experiences prolonged states of unrelieved stress is less able to accept comfort from caregivers or to turn to the world beyond the parent with curiosity and delight, less able to find relief and satisfaction through play.

Overcoming defensive adaptations that shape how children relate and respond to new adults in their lives takes much time and effort. The early years offer a window of opportunity when attachment diffi-culties can be addressed before they become entrenched. The encour-aging message from attachment research is that a child who has been able to form a close and loving relationship with consistent and reliable caregivers is likely to be more able to form trusting relationships with subsequent caregivers if there has to be a move.

## Protective factors

### Internal continuity

Attachment research shows that, in the same external situation, differ-ent children can have very different experiences. When attachment is secure, something inside the self that is felt to be nurturing and sup-portive helps the child to keep going when the parent is not present. Bowlby (1969) had the concept of an "internal working model", formed by expectations about caregivers derived from experiences in infancy that go on to shape relationships in later childhood and adult life. Mel-anie Klein, the first psychoanalyst to work with very young children, thought that during the first year of life, through repeated experience of being thought about and responded to, children form an "internal world" peopled by representations of parental figures which she called "internal objects" (Klein, 1958; see also Bower, 2005). In Klein's theory, healthy development depends on a helpful loving figure that has been taken inside the self. The idea of a mothering figure inside the self is illustrated by a toddler at nursery whom I overheard telling herself in a "mothering" tone of voice, "put my coat on and keep warm" as the children went outside to play. A good internal object allows emotions to be regulated and protects from the painful discontinuities described by Winnicott as gaps in "going-on-being" (1962, p. 61).

A child who has been unable to internalize a nurturing figure is more alone in his or her mind as well as in external reality. Parents usually introduce the world to their babies a little at a time, but a child who has been removed from his or her parents has crossed a basic divide into a world where everything is unfamiliar (Kenrick, Lindsey, & Tollemache, 2006; Rustin, 1999). A sense of internal continuity is more difficult to establish for children who have experienced early trauma, broken attachments, or a lack of close relationships with caregivers.

## Foster care

More positive outcomes have been consistently reported for children who remain in foster care or are adopted, compared with children who are returned to families where maltreatment has occurred (Berridge, 1997; Farmer & Lutman, 2010; Wade, Biehal, Farrelly, & Sinclair, 2010; Ward, Brown, Westlake, & Munro, 2010; Ward, Munro, & Dearden, 2006).

> The reality is that fostering is a success story. The research is clear, and has established, that for some decades now, children have entered care with serious problems, but that in general their welfare improved over time . . .
>
> [O]verall, children's views about fostering are remarkably positive. Although they have strong views on how and why fostering could be improved, their overall sense of well-being is surprisingly high. [Narey & Oates, 2018, p. 9]

This is the conclusion of a Department for Education review of foster care which drew on research by the Hadley Centre for Adoption and Foster Care Studies at the University of Bristol on the views of children and foster carers. For some children, foster care brings the first experience of "having a proper family who care about me", who notice how the child is feeling and support the child's learning, friendships, and out-of-school activities. Many children show marked improvements in their physical health, stature, mood, relationships, and learning after entering care. The overwhelming majority of children and young people in care in a recent survey (Selwyn, Magnus, & Stuijfzand, 2018) reported that they trusted their carers and felt safe and loved in their placements. More children who remain in care or who are adopted achieve stability in adult life than do those who are returned to maltreating parents, or those who move in and out of care.

## Change upon change

Although foster care has been shown to provide more positive outcomes for children who have been abused in their families, a system that is responsible for the safety of thousands of children cannot provide the consistency of a well-functioning family. Many children in care are exposed to the impact of repeated cumulative disruptions through placement moves, multiple caregiving, and contact routines with birth family members that do not recognize developmental needs.

In 2016–17, almost half of children leaving care under the age of one year had two or more placements, while one in seven children had three or more placements (DfE, 2017). Children who have to assimilate a new environment and a new foster family, perhaps repeatedly, are living with "multiple families in mind" (Rustin, 1999). Each change of placement can re-trigger memories of earlier losses and compound the impact of early trauma, bringing the child into contact with new professionals who may be unfamiliar with the child's original context and relationships. Craven and Lee describe the compounding of stress, at its greatest in moments of transition, by the uncertainty that prevails in the lives of many foster children:

> [A]t each stage of development . . . family members have the task of adjusting to the . . . emotional climate within the family, boundaries, patterns of interaction and communication. The foster child is faced with the task of adjusting to these normative tasks while transitioning to a new home environment . . . the foster child is unsure of his or her future and lives in a world of uncertainty. [2006, p. 288]

Children's relationships with their social workers are crucially important both for their understanding of why they are in care and for their development and stability during the upheavals of life in care (Bower, 2005). The specialist nature of the social work tasks of each aspect of the care system means that most infants in care experience changes of social worker as well as changes of foster carer. The high turnover of social workers and reliance on agency staff, stemming in part from extreme workloads and stress levels in children's services, also has a bearing on the many changes of social worker for most children in care. Trust becomes harder to achieve with each change (Selwyn, Magnus, & Stuijfzand, 2018). For a child who remains in care, there may be no adult still present in his or her life who can corroborate memories and experiences. The main facts are recorded, but the detail of the child's early experiences may become blunted with each change of social worker. What is lost is the experiential knowledge of the family and the child while they were together, who the child was in the family and what happened to him or her when first placed in care.

## Multiple caregiving

The impact of receiving care from different adults in the absence of a consistent figure holding the child in mind was explored in a series of ground-breaking films made by James and Joyce Robertson from the 1950s (Robertson & Robertson, 1952). The films stirred up much controversy but succeeded in radically altering practice in hospitals and residential nurseries in a way that repeated reports had failed to do: the visual medium of film seemed to make an impact that written accounts had not succeeded in creating. In *Separation and the Very Young* (1989), the Robertsons bring together their observations in a range of settings. A residential nursery is described where the children were well fed, clothed, and stimulated but were looked after by a frequently changing rota of staff. The impact on children, seen under the unflinching gaze of the camera, was profound. One child, who came to the nursery a few days old and was cared for by up to six nannies in a day, was silent and lethargic, developmentally delayed, and smiled indiscriminately. At 23 months, this child had long screaming episodes in which he could not be consoled by the staff. Another four and a half year-old child broke down with uncontrollable outbursts that required the nurses to hold him down to avoid his hurting himself and others.

The powerful impact of these films contributed to the development of the keyworker systems that are now the norm in nurseries and under-fives centres, while hospital policies now support parents remaining with their children wherever possible. But the Robertsons' descriptions of the effects of multiple caregiving remain relevant today. Indiscriminate smiling to strangers, artificial laughter, sudden mood swings, sudden aggression, increased motility, developmental delay, low tolerance of frustration, and prolonged and severe tantrums are frequently described in children who have experienced disruptions of their primary caregiving relationships, both before and after entering care.

Research on multiple caregiving shows that children in residential nurseries who do not have a relationship with an individual caregiver to whom they can become attached continually scan their environment for adult attention. Follow-up studies report that these children's development is more likely to be delayed; after they have been adopted, it is harder for them to cope with the ordinary comings and goings of family life (Rutter, 1998). Infants who have not formed attachments with adults are also less likely to have a special friend in early childhood, and thus are also less likely to benefit from the peer relationships that are significant protective factors against mental health difficulty during adolescence (Grossman, Grossman, & Waters, 2005).

## Transitions

Thousands of children move to live with a new family every year, but little systematic research has investigated this process and the experiences to which it gives rise. However, the largest study of adoption breakdown in the UK to date (Selwyn, Wijedasa, & Meakings, 2014) highlighted the significant adverse impact of poorly planned transitions. Abrupt or inadequately prepared placement moves were associated with greater risk of adoption breakdown.

In the practice guidelines in *A Child's Journey in Placement*, first published in the US in 1991, Vera Fahlberg emphasizes the importance of continuing relationships, especially for infants and young children. Direct and supportive contact between past and future carers plays a significant role in helping to create stability and security.

Also in the US, Clyman and Harden recommend that "continuing the relationship with the foster parents in a planful way after reunification may prevent the child from suffering another major loss" (2002, p. 444). In his paper "Undertaking Planned Transitions for Children in Out-of-Home Care", Andrew Browning describes an approach developed with the Australian Childhood Foundation to reduce the stress of abrupt discontinuities:

> One such practice is the development of a gradual transition process that avoids dramatic discontinuities for the child. Part of this process involves the child having ongoing contact with the family from which he or she has moved, with this contact decreasing gradually. Another aspect of a successful transition is the development of a constructive relationship between the two families involved. If this can be created, a child is more likely to be emotionally held in the process. [2015, p. 51]

Studies in the UK that have explored ways of mitigating the profound impact of placement moves identify the need for feelings of loss, grief, and disorientation to be acknowledged and accepted alongside the feelings of excitement and hopefulness about a new family (Hindle, 2008; Lanyado, 2003). A study of placement moves by Sophie Boswell and Lynne Cudmore, carried out together with local authority social workers, found that the emotional experience of the child becomes less prominent in professionals' minds as the move comes closer:

> It is a highly anxious time for the adults, and in the grip of these anxieties they can lose sight of what is happening emotionally for the child. The children's outward compliance with the move and lack of obvious emotion at losing their carers can be interpreted as signs that they are "fine". [2014, p. 8]

Feelings of loss, for the child and the foster family, and the significance of their relationship tended to become lost to sight amid the excitement and relief of a move to a new family. Heightened anxiety among the adults created a collective "blind spot" that hampered the capacity to remain in touch with the more complex underlying feelings of all those involved. The authors argue that,

> [C]urrent procedures are out of synch with some of the fundamental principles established in attachment theory. . . . Ideally there should be an expectation that when babies and children are moved from foster carers to adoptive parents it should be done gradually, like a careful weaning, and that they should retain some sort of meaningful contact with these carers and their families. Such separations should be treated as emotionally significant for the child, whether the child concerned is able to show feelings of distress or not. [2014, p. 19]

The "clean-break" ethos that has been influential in adoption practice in many local authorities and adoption agencies is in stark contrast to these guiding principles. Strong feelings as well as logistical difficulties undoubtedly underlie placement moves implemented over a few days and with little or no contact arranged between the child and the foster carer after the move.

When carers have stayed in touch with their former foster children, this has often happened informally and "under the radar", rather than being explicitly supported by local authorities or agencies as an aspect of emotionally involved caregiving. For many carers who continue to send cards, receive news about the children, or talk or meet regularly with the adoptive family, the relationship with and knowledge about children they have cared for helps to sustain them and validates their place in children's lives. Mary Dozier and colleagues (Dozier & Lindhiem, 2006) reported that foster carers are less likely to withdraw emotionally from the child when there is an expectation that they will have a continuing role in children's lives after the move to adoption. Yet a study for the Social Care Institute for Excellence published the same year describes an "adoption triangle" of child, birth parent, and adoptive parent, without mentioning foster carers, either as attachment figures for the child or as the adults who play the greatest role in facilitating the transition to adoptive families (Rushton, 2007). This stance seems to reflect powerful trends to erase the significance of foster carers and what they do. Ian Sinclair (Sinclair, Gibbs, & Wilson, 2004, p. 169) observes that "interventions recognising the unique experience of foster children and foster family dynamics were found to be lacking in the current literature". In another study, foster care is described as "effaced" from much of the research and policy literature on children in care (Craven & Lee, 2006, p. 287).

Experiences and practices in relation to the move from foster care to adoption have been investigated systematically for the first time by Mary Beek and colleagues at the University of East Anglia (Beek, Neil, & Schofield, 2018) who have developed guidelines following interviews and discussions with adoptive parents, foster carers, social workers, and mental health clinicians across the UK. Core principles underlying the recommendations are that positive relationships formed in foster care pave the way for the child's adoptive relationships, and that continuity of environment and relationships support a child in building trust. The guidance identifies three important stages in the transition: before, during, and after the move. This involves a shift from the traditional focus on the introductions as the critical element of the move and places a new emphasis on the importance of overlap between the current and new carers for the child, allowing time for the two sets of adults to get to know each other before the details of the move are planned. The first stage, in which the adults get to know each other, creates a context for the move and prepares for later visits by foster carers after the move to reassure the child that he or she is remembered.

Recognizing that children do not always show their feelings in obvious ways, the guidance also makes suggestions about ways of coming together for professionals to think about how best to support the child in expressing both positive and more difficult feelings about leaving his or her foster family and joining the new family. The period following a move is also considered as part of the transition: visits to the child in his or her new home by the foster carer or foster family are recommended within a few days of the child's move wherever possible. The researchers emphasize that the principles that underlie child-centred moves from foster care to adoption apply equally when children are moved from short-term to long-term foster placements or to special guardianship placements.

## Contact routines

Contact with birth families also has the potential to expose babies and young children to stressful disruptions if contact arrangements do not take developmental needs into account. Each contact, which may occur up to six times a week, involves a transition between the contrasting environments of the foster family and the birth family. When contact goes well, there are opportunities for handover between parents, foster carers, and the contact supervisors. The transition for the child is mediated by the adults coming together and sharing information about the child's routines and current developments; possible changes in the routine of contact can be thought about from the child's point of view, prepared for, and reviewed. In contrast, when relationships are strained or acrimonious, if threats have been made towards foster carers, or the child's trust in his or her foster carers has been undermined, it may not be possible for the adults to come together to ensure a containing and safe experience for the infant (Neil & Howe, 2004). Contact supervisors ensure physical safety, but the psychological experience for an infant as he or she moves between adults who cannot safely be in the same room cannot be thought through. Unmediated moves between disconnected environments and caregivers may bring risks of re-traumatizing the babies and young children with the greatest need for consistency and containment.

In concurrency planning, babies are placed with foster carers who have previously been approved as adopters. If the baby is not returned to parents by the family courts, the baby remains with the carers who have been bringing him or her up. In this way concurrency planning protects the infants from further disruption of their attachments. This arrangement also provides opportunities to investigate the nature and impact of the high-frequency contact with birth parents that often precedes placement with concurrent carers. Jenny Kenrick (2009) interviewed adoptive parents about their experiences of taking their children to and from contact during their period in concurrency care. For most of the babies, contact with their parents five or six times a week often involved long journeys to and from the supervised contact centre. Some carers who described children in states of extreme distress, before, during, or after contact felt that the babies needed to have more of the quiet time at home that is the norm for most babies in ordinary families. There would be little or no time for recovery, however, because they usually had to be on the road again the next day. Infants who had been through a hospital detoxification from drugs at birth were felt to be particularly vulnerable: one carer felt strongly that a child who had been withdrawn from drugs had a particular need for calm and quiet times and a very consistent routine. But the only quiet times for this infant were at weekends. Some of the adoptive parents noticed that their child showed extra sensitivity to separation and change months or years after they had been adopted.

Researchers in Australia at the University of Melbourne studied the experience of 40 infants under the age of one year who had contact between four and seven times a week (Humphreys & Kiraly, 2011). A literature review revealed that little attention had been paid to the potential impact of contact for infants. Case-files audits showed that high-frequency contact does not make it more likely that children will be returned to their parents. The babies in this study had constant disruptions to their sleeping and feeding routines and repeated long journeys in the company of a succession of unfamiliar escorts and supervisors. Wide variety in the quality of care by the parents during contact was reported. Focus-groups discussions that were also part of the Australian study revealed deep divisions of opinion about contact: while legal professionals seemed to lack awareness of the disadvantages of repeated discontinuities in the care of infants, carers and social workers felt concerned but powerless about the distress and discomfort to which the babies were repeatedly exposed.

Experiences of change upon change for babies and young children in care, in the form of multiple caregiving, placement moves, and adult-centred contact schedules, increase the risks of present and future difficulty for children whose development may already be significantly compromised.

## The profound impact of absence of attachment

The absence of a close relationship with a caregiver is profoundly damaging for development. Children who have been unable to form close, meaningful relationships with the adults looking after them are likely to experience distress, with little or no prospect of comfort or reassurance.

> In choosing between the two evils of broken and interrupted attachments or an experience of emotional barrenness, the latter is the more harmful as it offers less prospect for normal character development . . . what helps the child to grow up normally is the painful, disturbing process of learning how to deal with such emotions. [Freud & Burlingham, 1944, p. 590]

Among the most significant factors that can impede intuitive recognition of a baby's fundamental needs for affection and attachment are delay, secondary trauma, and "under-involved" caregiving.

## Delays

The ideals of permanency and stability for children who are removed from their families are continually brought into question. The adverse impact of delays caused by "drift" in care proceedings was addressed in recent family justice reforms limiting the duration of care proceedings to 26 weeks. Previously, the average duration of care proceedings was 65 weeks. While the time limit has been largely successful—the average duration of proceedings is now around 30 weeks—the judicial reforms coincided with family court judgments that have had unintended outcomes, including "indications that judges are making different, 'lower tariff' orders, which fail to secure permanency for children" (Masson, 2016, p. 191). At the same time, there has been a reduction in placement orders, and decision-making for some young children has been delayed (Masson, 2016; National Adoption Leadership Board, 2014).

Long delays before a child's permanent placement is decided create protracted and stressful uncertainty and can result in "provisional states of mind" that are detrimental to development (Beckett & McKeigue, 2003; Hindle, 2007; Kenrick, 2010; Masson, Dickens, Bader, Garside, & Young, 2017). Janet Philps (2003, p. 13) describes the exposure to ongoing uncertainty as a "paradoxical experience of confinement in an unheld state" and links this experience to borderline states of mind in which everything seems unreal and relationships and learning are suspended.

## Secondary trauma

Living in close contact with children who have been subjected to abuse and neglect can result in secondary trauma (Bentovim, 1992). Looking after children who have experienced abuse and neglect can impact significantly on the capacities of carers to remain emotionally available, sensitive, and responsive.

> You never relax for a moment, you feel like something is going to hit you at any moment, your breathing gets quicker, you wake up at night, at the

same time you're always feeling you're not doing right by the children, whatever you do feels wrong, or not enough. You feel helpless.

The foster carer quoted above took part in a European exchange project about foster care. He eloquently describes the impact of living with children who had been physically and sexually abused while in the care of parents who were addicted to drugs. This foster carer's disturbed sleep echoes the sleeplessness of children who had had to become vigilant in order to protect themselves and their siblings.

Minimizing distress, rigid adherence to procedures, and concrete thinking that excludes meaning are characteristic features of secondary trauma (Halton, 1994, 2014). Working relationships may become authoritarian, and emotionally meaningful discussions may be avoided. The structures of reflective supervision and consultation, cohesive team-work, and having a boundaried role in which it is possible to be effective, can help to mitigate the impact of secondary trauma (Bloom, 2003).

Foster carers need consistent, emotionally alert support from their networks and employing agencies in order to sustain their capacity for receptiveness and empathy and to enable them to go on reaching out to the children in their care.

## Emotionally involved caregiving

> The ability to "keep the child in mind" can be eroded in challenging situations. [Onions, 2018, p. 252]

Many studies have identified "under-involved" foster care as a risk factor for mental health difficulty and for adoption breakdown (Hillen, Gafson, Drage, & Conlan, 2012; Schein, Roben, Costello, & Dozier, 2017; Selwyn, Wijedasa, & Meakings, 2014). Infants and young children who rarely experience being held in their carer's arms or on their lap are deprived of the physiological benefits of physical closeness as well as emotional security. Guidance by the National Institute for Health and Care Excellence (NICE) and the Social Care Institute for Excellence (SCIE) on promoting the quality of life of looked-after children and young people recommends that social workers and foster carers encourage "warm and caring relationships between child and carer that nurture attachment and create a sense of belonging so that the child or young person feels safe, valued and protected" (NICE/SCIE, 2010, p. 18). Hardy and colleagues (2013) found that children in care are likely to receive less physical affection than children in birth families. In their paper, "'She was a foster mother who said she didn't give cuddles: the adverse early foster care experiences of children who later struggle with adoptive family life", Sarah Meakings and Julie Selwyn (2016) identify "cold, clinical care" in foster placements as a risk factor for adoption breakdown. In an independent review of foster care for the Department for Education, Narey and Oates (2018, p. 42) express concern about beliefs that physical affection is professionally discouraged for foster carers.

The task of providing affectionate, involved foster care is conflicted and profoundly demanding, as we see in Hogarth's sensitive portrayal of Moses (Figure 1 in the Introduction). The foster mother's readiness to step back as the child moves on, while at the same time remaining available and providing a background of love and security, comes at a cost (Nutt, 2006). During care proceedings or when a move to new caregivers is planned for a child, there may be less explicit acknowledgment among professional networks of the significance of the care and nurture provided by the foster family, potentially leaving foster carers feeling isolated and unsupported in crucial aspects of their roles. If adequate support and training are not in place, anxieties that may lead a foster carer to doubt the importance of his or her relationship for the child may also result in the foster carer withdrawing from the child (Dozier et al., 2009).

Advocacy for the emotional and relational dimensions of fostering is needed in order to promote caring environments that support carers to remain emotionally available to the children in their care (Lobatto, 2016). An organizational culture that does not fully acknowledge emotional realities in the life of children would leave carers with uncertainty about how much they can and should feel committed and close to the child in their care. Living with and trying to making sense of the complex and at times distressing feelings of vulnerable young children requires the commitment of a team around the child that supports the foster carer and validates the caregiving relationship.

## Witnessing

> Witnessing . . . may seem quite a modest function, [but] it has profound implications on an existential level. [Rhode, 2007, p. 208]

A continuing relationship with a reliable adult is the most crucial factor for recovery from trauma. A member of the extended family, a family friend, a foster carer, social worker, or teacher can provide a lifeline for a child, giving the child the experience of being noticed, taken seriously, and remembered.

When relationships have been marked by conflict, violence, or neglect, or when there have been repeated disruptions of a child's attachments, the early years provide the greatest opportunities for repair and recovery. Guidance by NICE and SCIE on promoting the quality of life of looked-after children and young people (NICE/SCIE, 2010) recommends that carers and frontline practitioners working with babies and young children receive specialist training on the development of attachment in infancy and early childhood, the impact of broken attachments, early identification of attachment difficulties, and the particular needs of babies and young children who have experienced prenatal substance exposure or who have inherited or acquired learning or developmental problems. Multi-agency trainings provide valuable opportunities for coming together to think about the emotional and psychological experiences and needs of young children, and the impact that they may have on the adults closest to them.

Interventions for children with developmental, emotional, or behavioural difficulties converge on the key concepts of child-led play and undivided attention from the caregiver. In speech and language therapy, parents, caregivers, and teachers are trained to support child-led play in order to increase opportunities for dialogue and moments of mutually enjoyable interaction. There is a focus on responding to the child as a person whose communications have meaning and who is looking for meaning. Intentionality and mind-mindedness also underpin the Secure Base training developed by Gillian Schofield and colleagues at the University of East Anglia:

> Key to promoting security and resilience is mind-mindedness—thinking about what is in the mind of the child. [Schofield & Beek, 2018]

Promoting play that is led by the child with undivided attention from an adult has been found in studies carried out in many countries to enhance children's confidence, coordination, imagination, and concentration. In the 1940s, the Hungarian paediatrician Emmi Pikler took over the running of a children's home at Lóczy, where she drew on systematic observation to research the interaction of infant motor development and spontaneous child-led play. The key principles that she identified of providing the caregiver's full, undivided attention and promoting free imaginative play remain influential in residential care and children's centres across Europe (Vamos, Tardos, Golse, & Konicheckis, 2010). The American child-development researcher Arietta

Slade sees child-led play as the means to consolidation and integration: in putting experiences and feelings into play, "the child is creating structure" (Slade, 1994, p. 91). Later studies have reported improvements in the communication between child and caregiver, and in the caregiver's attunement and sensitivity (Ayling & Stringer, 2013; Panksepp, 2007; Sunderland, 2007).

In the "Watch Wait and Wonder" model (Muir, 1992), the parent–infant therapist encourages parents to facilitate child-led play and reflect with the therapist on possible meanings of the play. Parenting programmes address the topic of attending to and commenting on child-led play, while the Solihull Approach integrates these concepts into health visiting practice (Briskman & Scott, 2012; Milford, Kleve, Lea, & Greenwood, 2006; Pallet, Blackeby, Yule, Weissman, & Scott, 2000; Solihull Approach, 2018). In the US, Attachment and Biobehavioral Catch-up (ABC; Dozier et al., 2009; Schein et al., 2017) has been developed as an individualized training programme in which foster carers and parents are trained to notice and respond to the smallest cues from children who may reject adult attention. In Africa, studies of children recovering from malnourishment report reduced mortality and increased speed of recovery in children who received intensive feeding and psychosocial support, in the form of promoting play and focusing attention on the child, compared to children who received intensive feeding only (WHO, 2004). A focus on psychological well-being was found to be critical in generating life-giving emotional connectedness between children and their caregivers.

The interventions described in this book explore the impact of being seen and of seeing oneself reflected in the eyes of another, for children and for the professionals working to support them.

# CHAPTER TWO

# Therapeutic observation

Observational skills are central to clinical work, as they are in many scientific and artistic endeavours. Psychoanalytic infant observation offers a way of developing these skills in the context of a weekly visit to observe a baby or young child in his or her family context and in the course of the family's usual routines and activities. The observer pays close attention to the fine detail of interactions and communications, together with the emotional responses that are evoked in the observer (Waddell, 2006; Wittenberg, 1999). Introduced by Esther Bick into the training of child psychotherapists at the Tavistock during the 1940s, this way of learning about child development and the heightened feelings evoked by the growing infant has become part of mental health and social care trainings throughout the world. Parkinson, Allain, and Hingley-Jones highlight the value of infant observation in social care and health trainings:

> Psychoanalytic baby observation is identified as a means for preparing practitioners to come close to and learn to tolerate, painful states of mind in individuals and their carers; to think deeply about those states and, in discussion with others, to articulate and respond to them. [2017, p. 11]

In their book *Learning Through Child Observation*, Fawcett and Watson (2016, p. 15) comment on the wider applications of observational skills to professional roles:

> The ability to observe effectively, to focus systematically in an open-minded manner is a skill that, once learned, has relevance far beyond the immediate event and contributes to ongoing professional competence with children.

## Psychoanalytic infant observation

> Psychoanalytically informed observation is a medium through which our hearts and minds can become more in touch with each other; it provides a space in which the observer is required to be fully present to the moment and is an activity that affords time to *feel* in order to *think*—to make careful and attentive connections. [Ruch, 2017, p. 7]

A search for psychological meaning in the earliest stages of life underpins the approach to infant observation that has become established in psychoanalytic trainings (Miller, Rustin, Rustin, & Shuttleworth, 1989; Reid, 1997; Trowell & Rustin, 1991). Bick was a child psychoanalyst who studied infant development in Vienna during the 1930s. Drawn to the tradition developed in Austria of paying close attention to every detail of the observed infant's movements, she began to look for an approach that could also encompass emotional experience, placing particular emphasis on fluctuations in the feeling of being held together (1964, 1968). Her interest in infant observation was inspired by what she saw as the gathering effect of attention:

> Your attention to everything she does and everything she says acts like a magnet that draws together the fragments of her personality . . . a magnet drawing together iron filings . . . That is what a mother's attention also does for a baby. [personal communication, cited in Williams, 1998, p. 94]

Bick came to understand each aspect of physical care as having a psychic and emotional dimension: thinking about the baby was seen as the psychic equivalent to physical holding; talking to the baby and providing nurturing experiences as the mental equivalent of feeding; and containment, helping the baby to get rid of painful feelings, as the equivalent of cleaning (Haag, 2002; Rustin, 2009).

The "Tavistock model" of psychoanalytic infant observation established by Bick has three essential elements: the weekly, hour-long visit to the family at an agreed regular time, with short, pre-planned holiday breaks; a detailed record written after each visit which describes the sequence of the infant's movements, gestures, vocalizations, and interactions during the observation hour, and of any particularly striking emotional impact on the observer; and a weekly discussion in a seminar group.

The two-year duration of the observation for child psychotherapists in training is often shorter in other professional trainings. The observer is responsible for finding a family who agree to their baby or young child being observed; this needs to be a family with whom the observer has no social or professional relationship and with whom statutory social services are not involved. The idea is for the observer to learn as much as possible from the infant and his or her interactions, without the distractions of social conversation or the need to take up a professional role. The lack of a social or professional relationship also protects the confidentiality of the family.

Finding a family is usually done through an intermediary such as a health visitor or by making contact with local groups. Information about the training course and about how the observation is conducted is given to parents who express an interest in meeting to discuss the possibility of an observer visiting the family. Ideally, the observer and the parents meet before the baby is born, and the visits begin as soon after the birth of the baby as the family wish and feel is practicable.

Students take turns to read out and discuss their notes in a small seminar group of around five students. The observer is supported by the seminar group to learn from the challenges of observing with respect and self-containment, putting the family's needs and feelings before his or her own and interfering as little as possible in the family's routines (Daws, 1999). The focus of the seminar group discussion is on trying to understand what the baby may be experiencing and communicating; links are made with relevant child development research and psychoanalytic theory.

> Infant observation . . . is a learning experience that involves . . . deep emotional implications and contains an extraordinary maturational potential. [Maiello, 1997, p. 49]

Training in baby and young child observation was introduced to social work qualifying programmes in the 1980s and 1990s, as a response to criticisms in child death inquiries about social workers "apparently failing to 'see' the children they were supposed to be safeguarding (Tanner, 1999)" (Hingley-Jones, 2017, p. 31).

The observer is in the unique and privileged position of participating in the emotional intensity of infant development and the unfolding mother–baby and family relationships. Powerful feelings may be stirred up in proximity to a new life and by witnessing the absolute vulnerability and dependence of the infant. Learning to notice and pay attention to the whole range of emotions evoked by the infant is an important part of what makes infant observation a valuable training experience for work in mental health and social care (Le Riche & Tanner, 1998; Sternberg, 2005; Youell, 2005).

Although the main purpose of a training observation is the trainee's learning about child development, many families who have chosen to accept the offer of an observation have reported finding it helpful for themselves. Contained by the structure of the approach and by the seminar group, the observer may be able to carry a containing function for the family. The regular visit of an adult who is interested in every detail of the baby's life, and the impact of the baby on the whole family without being intrusive or didactic, can be welcome and reassuring. Some parents have commented that the observer's presence encouraged them to observe their growing infant more closely themselves (Watillon-Naveau, 2008). This recognition has led to the applied use of infant observation for therapeutic purposes (Urwin & Sternberg, 2012).

## Therapeutic observation

Therapeutic observation applies the principles of psychoanalytic infant observation to clinical contexts where there are concerns about a child's development, the relationship with the primary caregiver, or the impact of an impending transition to new carers (Rustin, 2014). The approach comprises the same core elements as an observation in training. The observational visit, arranged at a time convenient for the family, may be less frequent than once-weekly, but ideally it is scheduled for a regular time, and detailed notes written after each visit are discussed in supervision with an experienced practitioner.

A therapeutic observer takes up a more active role than an observer in training—drawing attention, for example, to gestures or sounds that might otherwise go unnoticed (Rhode, 2007). When there are breaks or ruptures in the connection between child and carer, a therapeutic observer tries to help them to re-connect, often by putting something into words but also simply by holding something in mind and reflecting on experiences of disconnection. Verbalizing a feeling or a wish that may have been overlooked can provide the reassurance that the child's signals can be seen and have meaning.

Feelings of connection can be supported when there is a separation by talking to the infant about the absent parent or carer, showing that they can be held in mind even when they are not present. By remaining interested and friendly, and maintaining the regularity of the visits wherever possible, the therapeutic observer may also carry the function of taking in unwelcome emotions: feelings of being excluded, rejected, or forgotten about may be passed on to the observer. When, with the help of supervision, the observer is able to accept and make sense of these non-verbal communications and to continue to be friendly and receptive, strong feelings can be contained and mitigated. This can provide an experience of emotional turmoil as potentially meaningful and as promoting growth.

Therapeutic observation is a planned intervention that sets out to explore identified concerns or difficulties, while maintaining the open-ended, exploratory quality of observations in training. The role of therapeutic observer draws on the skills of an experienced clinician with prior training in psychoanalytic observation. In this way it differs from what is sometimes called "participant observation", to denote a training observation in the course of which significant difficulties become apparent that warrant a more proactive stance from the observer (Blessing & Block, 2014).

Therapeutic observation has often been found helpful in circumstances where something has got in the way of the connection between a parent or primary caregiver and the baby. It offers an unintrusive approach with minimal disruption to family life (Houzel, 1999, 2008; Rustin, 2014, 2018; Wakelyn, 2012a, 2012b). An observation that continues over time allows the observer to become something of a companion to the child and his or her carer. A receptive, non-judgmental observer who visits regularly may become someone who can know about distress and difficulty for the family as well as share in moments of delight, relief, and celebration. An overview of interventions to support parent–infant relationships (Barlow & Svanberg, 2009) highlights the potential for the clinician's observational focus to activate and engage the observing part of the parent. An observer who remains actively interested in a baby, however fragile or disabled the baby may be, models curiosity and hopefulness in a way that can be encouraging for parents and professionals alike. For clinicians, the focus on trying to understand what the baby's experience might be like can help to find a position alongside parents and professionals without being experienced as critical or intrusive.

Observation-based approaches can offer a rewarding experience for clinicians, and much can be learned from this way of working. At the same time, therapeutic observation faces clinicians with the challenges of closer contact with infants and families in times of great distress and upheaval. Feeding back to and maintaining communication with professional networks to support a focus on the child is a part of the remit of the therapeutic observer that requires sensitivity and tact as well as persistence.

## Applications of therapeutic observation

In medical contexts where there are high levels of anxiety about an infant's well-being, or even survival, therapeutic observation may be supportive both for parents and for medical staff, forming an intervention in itself as well as informing further intervention (Fletcher, 1983; Geraldini, 2016; Mendelsohn, 2005).

> At its simplest, an active interest in the baby, no matter how premature, fragile or disabled, provides a model for both parents and staff. The curiosity aroused in those observing the observer often seems to act as a powerful catalyst for a new kind of way of looking at the infant, and consequently a new kind of interaction. . . . Parents can then begin to do the job, which they do naturally with older and fitter infants, of acting as an emotional container for their baby. Parents can be supported in this task, which is of course often a painful one when the child is in a life-threatening situation, by sensitive staff. If they are able to feel emotionally contained by the unit or by one or two people working in the unit, they will be able to respond far more sensitively to their child. [McFadyen, 1994, p. 164]

Applications of therapeutic observation with babies born prematurely have been explored by Romana Negri in Italy since the 1960s. Negri's background in neuropsychiatry led to interventions using groups of clinical observers in neonatal units that had measurable outcomes for the oxygen levels of the premature infants. A particular focus of the work was seen to be in the bringing together of fragmented emotional states evoked by the extreme vulnerability of the premature infant, putting those close to the premature infant into contact with "parts of ourselves [that] found it difficult to be psychologically born and to find their identity" (Negri, 1994, p. 81). Experiences of disorientation at the start of observational work with premature infants were also reported in a study by Ross Lazar and colleagues (1998) in Austria: the observers found themselves unable at first to look at the baby and, when they did look, unable to remember what they had seen. Bringing together small details that at first appeared to be without meaning or associated affect was found to be a particularly taxing aspect of this work.

> For, in the world of prematurity, things do not simply pop into one's mind, . . . as pictures, nor sounds, nor feelings . . . and certainly not as words! Instead, these must be searched for in a way much more akin to the way babies themselves seem to do it: that is by arduously gathering together various seemingly arbitrary bits and pieces of experience, tiny memory traces and the first suggestions of emerging patterns, relationships and potential consistency into tiny units of retainable memory. [Lazar & Ermann, 1998, p. 23]

Anne Alvarez comments that on hearing the observer's descriptions, "One really got a sense of what it could be like, at the very start of extra-uterine life, not to be able to take even breathing for granted" (2000, p. 104). It was striking that the observer felt no distress while in the presence of the baby, only coming into contact with painful emotions as her thoughts and reflections were brought together in discussions with the group. The containment and reflection together with the group with whom the observations were discussed were essential for the observer to be able to think.

Therapeutic observation is used as part of multidisciplinary interventions in child psychiatry services in France, often when there are concerns about early signs of autism or significant difficulties in the parent–child relationship (Dugnat & Arama, 2001; Houzel, 1999, 2008). The visits of the therapeutic observer are seen as containing parental anxiety and distress as well as enhancing the parents' own sense of their competency. Delion (2000) describes the evolution of observational approaches from the conviction that prompt discovery of signs of risk followed by early and sustained specialist intervention can considerably modify outcomes for a baby at risk of developing social communication difficulties. Dugnat (2001) emphasizes the role of attentive observation in bringing together different professionals and services and in facilitating collective reflection in teams.

In the UK, Maria Rhode has written about interventions for young children at risk of being diagnosed with autism later in childhood (2007). The intervention usually consists of weekly visits by an experienced observer for one year, together with fortnightly parental-support sessions with another worker for the mother, or, where possible, both parents. Some of the parents also accessed individual therapy for themselves. A pilot trial demonstrated encouraging outcomes following the intervention. Young children who show signs of possible autistic difficulties may have difficulties in tuning in to other people, which can make parents or professionals feel redundant. When hopefulness has been undermined, it becomes much harder to notice and respond to the child's signals. A vicious circle in which both child and parents withdraw can then add to existing problems in relating. Rhode (2007) suggests that the presence of a sensitive observer who is able to be engaged without becoming intrusive may be particularly helpful in situations where parents have come to lack confidence in interacting with their child. As Berta and Torchia (1998) highlight, the focus in the observational approach on making links and looking for meaning in the smallest gestures or glances can help to maintain a hopeful stance that gives time for infant and caregiver to find each other. For the parent–child dyads in this study, being helped to have experiences of more enjoyable and more consistent interaction seemed to create the conditions for relationships and development to get back on track.

Observational interventions to support infants with physical illness and their families have also been described. Monica Cardenal (1999) carried out a therapeutic observation with a baby who had experienced the medical trauma of anaesthetics, injections, and radiotherapy for cancer of the retina in his fourth month. This intervention included meetings with the parents to discuss and share observations. Bianca Lechevalier and colleagues described the observation-based treatment of a baby who developed features of West's syndrome, a neuro-convulsive disorder of infancy, in the context of traumatic family conflicts. Aged three and a half, the child was in good health and meeting developmental milestones; at five, he integrated successfully at nursery. The authors suggest that "therapeutic infant observation of mother and baby together at home opens up a containing space . . . and helps integrate emotions" (Lechevalier, Fellouse, & Bonnesoeur, 2000, p. 28). They also highlight links between professionals including the paediatrician, the child psychiatrist, and the observer that helped the mother to feel supported at times of particular depression and anxiety.

Therapeutic observation has also been used to support young children living in institutions. In a Russian orphanage for children with neurological disorders, Marina Bardyshevsky describes an eleven-month-old infant about whom staff were particularly worried (1998). Having experienced numerous separations before coming to the orphanage, his motor development was severely delayed, he made no eye contact, he did not vocalize, and he was unresponsive to his carers' attempts to interact with him. Encouraging changes were seen over the fourteen months of the observational intervention: he became interested in toys, engaged in face-to-face interaction, and began to seek and accept comfort from an adult. Alongside these developments, a rapid development was seen in his motor skills.

In a residential nursery for profoundly deprived children in Hungary, Erzsebet Tarsoly (1998) also found that observing the children alongside the carers and reflecting together on their observations helped to promote more individual and attuned relationships between the staff and the children. Tarsoly comments on how the capacity to provide consistent loving care can be adversely impacted by high ratios of children to staff and rigid institutional regimes.

### Observational approaches with babies and young children during care proceedings

Like premature infants, children in care may have experienced the basic trauma of moments when they have been unable to take survival for granted from one minute to the next. Episodes of acute terror, more or less extended periods in which their basic needs are neglected, and repeated changes of primary caregiver leave children in a world that is precarious and fragmented. Gillian Miles describes a year of observational visits in five different households to "Kerrie", who was cared for by each of her teenage parents, and then by different members of her extended family, before being placed in foster care when she was fifteen months old. The observer provided a thread of continuity as Kerrie moved between foster homes and her parents, despite sudden, unprepared moves from one environment to another that threatened to interrupt the observer's visits (Bridge & Miles, 1996, p. 95). The observer's background presence and the focus that she maintained on the child in the different settings seemed to help the parents and foster carers to link up to share worries and their understanding of Kerrie's needs.

Jackie Hall (2009) describes an intervention using therapeutic observation during care proceedings that resulted from concerns about domestic violence. This intervention followed the teenage mother and her baby from a mother–baby foster placement to life in independent accommodation. An encouraging early sign was the interest the baby's mother took in the observations. As the intervention continued, the mother's relationships with professionals improved, and the social worker, the mother, and the observer began to be able to join together to think about the needs of the one-year old infant.

The focus in psychoanalytic infant observation on the slow gathering of impressions and on the meaning and impact of early experiences and relationships seems to fit well with the life circumstances of infants and young children in care. In the next chapters, I describe research exploring the application of this model with babies and young children in foster care and service developments drawing on insights from observation-based therapeutic work.

# CHAPTER THREE

# Clinical research: therapeutic observation with an infant in foster care

During my training as a child and adolescent psychotherapist, I had the valuable opportunity to take part in a research programme exploring the use of therapeutic observation with infants at risk of developing autistic spectrum difficulties (Rhode, 2007). Therapeutic observation sets out to address areas of development or interaction that are causing concern, alongside the overall aim of providing a deeper understanding of the child's relationships, experiences, and needs. The profound changes that were seen in the children and in the parent–child dyads after one year of observational support inspired me to explore the possibility of applying this way of working with young children in care. Thousands of children move to live with a new family every year, but this experience has rarely been the subject of research. My role as a child psychotherapist in a specialist mental health service for children in care provided an opportunity to carry out clinical research exploring the possibility of offering therapeutic observation with a baby in foster care (Wakelyn, 2011, 2012a, 2012b).

At the time I began my research, few studies had been published about the lives of babies and young children in care. In clinical work with children and teenagers who have been adopted or who have remained in long-term foster care, often little or nothing is known of their history before they came into care or about their significant relationships with foster carers and social workers. I hoped that the research would help me to understand more about the early experiences of a baby in the care system, and of his or her foster carers and social workers. Another aim of the study was to generate ideas that could be investigated in further research. If the baby was to be adopted, I hoped to meet his or her adoptive parents and to explore the possibility of continuing the observation in the adoptive home.

Despite its fundamental significance for clinical work, this seemed a difficult topic to approach. As the project took shape, I noticed that I became more anxious about coming closer to the experiences of a baby who had experienced loss and disruption, perhaps feeling that too much had already been exposed for such an infant. I felt uncertain, too, about how my role would be understood, what would be asked of me, and how I should conduct myself in the new situation of being a regular visitor to a foster home. This was the beginning of an exploration that took me into the life of the baby I call Rahan and his foster family. The research took me on an illuminating journey that has informed the development of services for babies and young children in care and the wider work of a multidisciplinary team.

Discussions with local authority social workers and social work managers were part of the preparation for the study. After ethical approval for the study was obtained from the local authority and the Research Ethics Committee, I met with the supervising social workers, whose role is to support and manage foster carers, to introduce the ideas behind the research. I had anticipated that it might take a long time to find a foster family and social workers who would agree to the research, but the project was welcomed by the social workers and fostering managers, who hoped that it would contribute to trainings for professionals and prospective adopters. I met Rahan's foster carer, whom I call Nadira, and she and her family agreed to take part in the project. Nadira had been caring for Rahan since birth. He was almost two months old when I first visited, and I went on to visit him once a week in the foster home for ten months. To my regret, it did not prove possible for me to meet the adoptive family or to continue the observation in his new home, but I continued to visit Nadira and her family for four months after he was moved away.

## Rahan

Rahan had been placed with Nadira and her family on the day of his birth. His teenage mother, "Tamara", had decided to give him up to be adopted, expressing only her wish for him to be adopted by a Muslim family. Tamara had sought help from social services for support when her boyfriend became violent towards her. When she found out that she was pregnant, she returned to her family. Her pregnancy was concealed from the religious community of her family. Social workers feared for her safety and visited her in the family home to offer continuing support, which she declined to take up. Tamara left the hospital a few hours after Rahan was born; on the same day he was brought to the foster home by Nadira, who looked after him until he was adopted. Anxieties about Tamara's safety continued to preoccupy her baby son's social worker.

This is a relatively rare situation in the care system today. Rahan had the stability of a single foster placement, and there was no contact between Rahan and his mother or with her family. From the point of view of the research, this provided a rare opportunity to focus on the experience of growing up in a nurturing but temporary relationship in foster care. Rahan may have been exposed in the womb to the stress of his mother's fears and anxieties, and he experienced the trauma of separation from his mother on the day of his birth, but there was no maltreatment or change of primary caregiver.

The research gave me the opportunity to experience the unfolding of intimate and loving relationships in the foster family over the ten months of the observation. I was also able to take part to some degree in the uncertainties, anxieties, and hopes that accompanied his adoption. At the end of the research project, I met participants to receive and offer feedback: they included Nadira, her supervising social worker, Rahan's social worker, the social work team manager, and the independent reviewing officer. We were able to discuss how I had conducted the study and how learning from the research could contribute to training and service development. I was pleased to hear from Nadira and the local authority social workers that they were in favour of sharing the findings from the research, in suitably anonymized form, to help us better understand the needs of infants in care and of the foster carers looking after them.

The research data, consisting of notes on the observations, my supervisions, and notes on meetings with professionals during the project, were analysed using grounded theory, a qualitative research methodology that is widely used in child psychotherapy and social sciences research (Glaser & Strauss, 1967; Rustin, 2001, 2012; Rustin & Rustin, 2019). The method aims to produce "rich description", conveying something of the depth and detail of interactions. As in infant observation itself, grounded theory involves an attitude of receptive openness to new connections: "constant comparison" is used in reading through data to uncover recurrent themes or underlying categories and to generate hypotheses and questions (Anderson, 2006; Holton, 2007).

What follows in this chapter is an account of the observational visits and discussions with social workers during the ten months of the observation.

## Beginnings

Rahan's foster carer, Nadira, and her husband, Daamin, have three children of their own. When I visit to introduce myself to Nadira and the foster family, I feel that I am expected: Kemal, their eleven-year-old son, greets me at the door and gestures with a friendly smile towards the kitchen. I take off my shoes and follow him to the kitchen. I find Nadira holding the seven-week-old Rahan in her lap. Although the purpose of this visit was to meet Nadira and explain what the therapeutic observation research would involve and ask if she would like to consider taking part, something had already begun in the very first moment of our meeting.

> Nadira, a serious-looking, attractive young woman with shining dark hair, gives me a warm smile. Lying in her lap, Rahan is staring at the wall behind her as he sucks on the bottle. His face has the look of a little old man, sunk into himself; his large features, long eyebrows, and prominent nose somehow seem not joined up. I feel sad and guilty about my instant thought that he is an ugly baby and feel scared by the idea of observing him.
>
> Nadira talks to Rahan in a gentle, soothing voice. After a few minutes, she puts him into a car seat near her on the floor. When he starts to cry, she gives him a toy which he does not seem to see. I ask Nadira if he has a favourite toy. She says, "All toys are the same to him . . . and anyway, he can't hold on." She rocks the car seat with her foot and tells me that they decided as a family to try fostering, to see how they got on with it.
>
> A little later, there is a sense of still-raw shock as she tells me about a phone call from someone she didn't know, just after she had been approved as a foster carer, telling her to collect a baby from the hospital the next day. At the hospital they asked her to wait outside while they checked her identification, and then they passed the baby to her at the door of the ward. On the way home she worried that someone would be waiting to fight her or take the baby.

As she tells me about their first moments together, Rahan begins to cry. She lifts him up and holds him close, then lays him on the blanket and talks to him soothingly. His face lights up and his whole body quivers, he stretches up his arms and legs and face towards Nadira.

She describes the first week with him. As I look at Rahan, listening to Nadira, the lilting tone of her voice, I am surprised and moved to see that he seems to come together; he looks more connected, his face and eyes have more colour. I feel drawn to him, and more hopeful. Nadira looks at him closely and murmurs tenderly, "Shall we sing to Jenifer? She hasn't heard you sing yet." It feels like a quiet celebration.

Nadira's idea of singing has the quality of a celebration, marking the coming together between herself and Rahan. This seems to help him to become more joined up, as if coming together with himself; he seems more integrated and more present. I also feel welcomed myself, as if our coming together in this new project is also being quietly celebrated.

When I meet Rahan's social worker to discuss the research with her, I am struck by the complex connections she has been able to hold in mind. She recalls that Tamara told her that she found herself thinking about Rahan most in the early evening, and she adds that Nadira told her that Rahan seemed to have a particular way of crying just at this time and that the foster family had wondered if this was when his mother was thinking about him. There seems to be a very strong wish in those around Rahan to hold on in mind to any possible connection with his mother. At the same time, the fact of his separation from his mother on the day of his birth is stark and seems to be reflected in the unmediated way in which he was "collected" by Nadira from the hospital. It also resonates in the unmediated nature of our first meeting, when there is a feeling of something very powerful happening with great suddenness, and no one there to mediate the intensity or introduce us. When Nadira speaks gently to Rahan about singing for me, I feel that something new is happening. A livelier atmosphere evolves when turmoil and anxieties that seemed to be being relived are put into words: as past and present become differentiated, a more hopeful idea of the future comes into mind. The baby who "can't hold on" becomes the baby who will be able to sing.

In my second visit, I meet Nadira's husband, Daamin. He tells me that he thinks it is wrong that Rahan will be adopted just when he is starting to crawl; in his view, children should have at least two years with a family before they have to move. Nadira says it will be difficult at any time, at any age. She holds Rahan and smiles at her husband and me, as if feeling supported by knowing that the painfulness and difficulty can be recognized. Rahan's social worker and Nadira let me know that they agree to take part in the research, and the observation begins.

Nadira kneels next to Rahan and kisses him on both cheeks; he moans, and then is very still. She lies down close to him and says she doesn't know what he wants right now. Is he hungry? Or sleepy? She looks at him, wondering. I ask what has been happening for Rahan. She asks if I mean about the adoption, and says it is a long process. Finding a culturally matched family could take a long time and could mean him moving out of London. Then he would be "really lost": away from his mother and away from them. She says she tells them that she has to feel he is hers, she looks after him as if he were hers, babies can tell, they need you to feel they're yours, with all the love and passion you have with your own children.

She tells me they wanted to adopt him themselves, but they were told he would have to have his own room, not share like their children do. She was told "you would not be the first choice". She says the social workers keep telling her, "remember he is not yours". Rahan begins to whimper as Nadira tells me his social worker tells her she should not look after him the same way she looked after her own babies . . . there are things she has to do differently, like how she gives him his bath. I say it feels a lot to take.

She turns back to Rahan, who has been looking up at the ceiling. She asks him, "What do you see up there?" She tries the bottle again, and this time he takes most of it, sucking strongly. There is a sense of tension dropping away. He has a good feed and holds the teat in his mouth as she holds him in her arms. After a while he stops sucking and holds the teat in his mouth; he looks at her languorously as she says quietly: "Drink now, then you can play."

After a while she lifts him, cradles him in her arms, and takes him to look with her in the mirror. He looks at the reflection and makes a plaintive sound. She murmurs, "What is it, what's wrong? Jenifer is here to see you; you will get to know Jenifer." She puts him in the Moses basket and wraps a blanket around him. His eyes slowly close as he rubs the back of his hand against his cheek and slowly his thumb finds its way into his mouth. Observation 1 (3 months, 1 week)

I felt grateful for Nadira's welcome and her openness. She introduces me to Rahan and helps me to feel that my role is accepted and valued.

As in my first visit, there was a feeling of marking a beginning in a way that felt different from the unmediated first coming together between Rahan and Nadira. I notice how Nadira articulates the idea of sequence for Rahan, differentiating between present and future: *"Drink now, then you can play."* With the sense of sequence, time mediates between the unknown and the known: *"you will get to know Jenifer."*

When Rahan touches his cheek with his hand he is echoing Nadira stroking his face, her kisses, and the caress of her gaze on his face. He seems to have taken something in from her that allows him to find his thumb, and he settles. There is a feeling that something good can be taken inside, both the milk and the loving care and attention he receives from his foster mother. He is protected and buffered from the jarring message given to Nadira, *"remember he is not yours"*.

The rhythm of the weekly visit takes some weeks to become established. In the first observations, I find it difficult to work out where to put myself. After the visit, I find it hard to bring my thoughts together. Writing the notes takes several hours and leaves me physically and mentally exhausted. All my energy seems to go into absorbing, receiving, and gathering feelings and impressions and maintaining the continuity of the observation. It was only in talking with my supervisor that I could begin to make connections and think. The regular routine of Nadira's prayer helps to provide a sense of structure.

Nadira is sitting on the edge of the bed leaning over Rahan, who is propped up on a cushion and looking up at her. She invites me to sit on a chair near the bed. She looks into his face as she holds the bottle. He looks raptly into her eyes while sucking hard on the bottle; she talks to him quietly, in a high voice, their faces quite close. I look at his large hands, resting on hers.

Nadira picks him up and rubs his back with steady circular movements. He blinks and looks in my direction, his eyes unfocused. I say to him quietly, "Hello Rahan, I have come to see you again today". He looks at me steadily with his large grey eyes, turns his head and smiles into Nadira's shoulder, looks at me again and smiles, looking towards me. I am taken aback by his ready smile. I repeat my quiet "Hello". Now he whimpers and moans, his body tenses and he begins to hiccup, then his hiccups alternate with little cries. He glances at me and away again, writhes and reddens.

I feel I am sitting too close, just a few feet away from the bed, and move back a little. Nadira soothes him, the hiccups subside. She holds him close, he blinks and looks at me steadily, smiles into her shoulder. He looks at me again and smiles.

She lays him on the floor and gives him a soft toy to hold, explaining to him and to me that she is going to pray now. He drops the toy. She kneels and leans over him and strokes his face, then continues her prayer. I feel moved that her prayer includes him. He turns his head and brings his knees up, flailing his arms and legs for a few moments before touching his cheek with the back of his left hand. Gradually his thumb goes into his mouth, and when he really sucks on it he relaxes, his eyes unfocused. Observation 2 (3 months, 2 weeks)

Connected with her community and her spirituality through her religious belief and practice, Nadira is able to remain connected with Rahan during her prayer. As he strokes his cheek and takes his thumb in his mouth, he is able to join up with himself and become more able to wait.

In most of my visits, although I hear about busy times with the children at breakfast and after school, and their lively interest in Rahan, the house is quiet during the day. I feel that my presence is accepted by Nadira as she continues her household routines and shares her observations of Rahan with me. He is held in Nadira's gaze and voice as she helps him to join up his left and right side, and his head with his body, in the game of "Round and Round the Garden".

Nadira talks to Rahan and turns him round so I can see him, kisses him, and strokes his cheek. She tells me she is worried that he only turns to the left, so much so that his head is flat on one side. She encourages him to turn towards me, on his right. He turns a little, then turns his face all the way back to the left, towards the wall. Then he looks into her face. She kisses his chin and plays "Round and Round the Garden", touching his tummy, arms, and face in time with the song. His gaze becomes lively and focused. He looks at me with bright eyes, and I feel he is seeing me for the first time today. Observation 2 (3 months, 2 weeks)

Nadira tells me I will meet her children at half term. She says they know about my visits and what I am doing. This is helpful for me, but nevertheless a worry comes into my mind that the change in the routine means I will forget to visit for the observation. When I arrive at the usual time and Kemal answers the door and tells me that Nadira has taken Rahan out, I feel confused and upset. I am vividly put in touch with Nadira's experience of a baby who could disappear at any moment.

When I return half an hour later, Nadira is outside the house. She tells me she has just got back from the shops and greets me warmly.

> As she takes Rahan out of the buggy, I comment on how much he has grown in just a week. Nadira reminds me of his turning to the left. She is intrigued when I say it seems that people often hold babies on their left side where the baby can hear their heart beating. She holds him to her left shoulder and looks into the mirror with him. His gaze becomes lively and focused. He looks at me. I feel he is now seeing me for the first time today, and I greet him. Observation 3 (3 months, 3 weeks)

When I arrive for the fourth observation, Nadira is talking to her mother on the phone. I realize that this is the first time since my first visit that I am seeing Rahan in her lap. He takes hold of a duck-shaped cushion that has belonged to each child in the family in turn.

> Nadira is talking on the phone to her mother in her home country. Rahan is in her lap; her arm is firmly around him, and he leans back into her breast. He looks warm and relaxed, his eyes are dark and shining. He looks towards me, waves his arms, and kicks out with his legs.
>
> They are both wearing dark blue; Nadira is wearing pyjamas and a warm dressing gown, Rahan a fleecy all-in-one. She tells me he had a very long sleep, and did not wake up once since about ten last night. Yesterday he also slept for a long time. She wonders if it is because of the cold and dark. I remember my long sleep after the first observation.
>
> She gives him a yellow duck-shaped cushion that has a soft orange beak and eyes. He takes hold of it with both hands and nuzzles his mouth into it, clamping it in his jaws.
>
> Later, as she leans over the cot to feed him, he sucks quietly and regularly . . . lying still, he holds and gently touches her hands, then drops his hands back by his head. He repeats this sequence of movements again and again. Nadira shows me some marks on his head that she thinks are from forceps or suction when he was born, she is not sure. She looks at him in a wondering way and strokes his head. She tells me he came with nothing from his mother; all that she has been able to keep for him is his hospital wristband.
>
> As Nadira kneels to pray next to Rahan in the baby bouncer, he half turns towards her, then towards me, then turns his head round to stare at a picture, a sticker of a girl singer's face on chest of drawers belonging to Dina (Nadira's youngest daughter); his gaze locks on to the picture.

Telling me about the psychologist who came to visit, and commented on the pleasure of seeing a baby doing so well, Nadira wonders how he is really doing—compared to other babies. She says, "Well—for now he is well." Observation 4 (4 months)

Nadira has the containment of her mother's attention and interest, while I am sustained by the regular rhythm that has begun to be established and by my clinical supervision. Held in our joint attention, Rahan is given a transitional object that he holds tight. Absorbent, soft, with a history of belonging to the family baby, this proto-toy, halfway between cushion and toy, can be embraced, nuzzled into, bitten, embraced, gripped, dropped, and retrieved.

The family's own plans and needs remain on hold during the thirteen months of the foster placement. They cannot go on a holiday together because Rahan's adoption is felt to be always imminent.

Nadira tells me how much she would like to bring Rahan to her home country to see her mother. But the social workers said they cannot take him on holiday because "he could go at any time". Observation 4 (4 months)

It is unthinkable for this foster family to let Rahan be placed with other carers while they have a holiday.

## Development accompanied by foreboding

The middle period of the observation is marked by waiting and uncertainty. Each developmental step forward for Rahan seems to bring closer the painful reality of the time when he will be taken away, and the foster family have no idea if they will ever see him again. There are bleak feelings of sameness, monotony, and futility.

Rahan is lying on a pillow in the middle of the bed, sucking quietly at the bottle that Nadira is holding for him. He holds one of her hands and looks at her intently. She strokes his legs gently and reminds me how ill he was last week, how unhappy and unsettled he was, and how much attention he had needed then, day and night.

Nadira wonders aloud whether she would do this again. She reminds me that she hasn't yet met any other foster carers.

Rahan looks toned and alert while she is speaking near him, then slumps and protests when she leaves the room. When she comes back, she wipes the bedside table with a cloth in a half-hearted way. Rahan begins to cry. She shows me his bottle and says, "They leak, the social workers buy the cheapest ones." She says to him, "This is what they got you." I feel surprised and sad to learn that she doesn't buy his bottles.

While he sleeps she tells me she knows he will be adopted, he will go. She has accepted it, and she thinks they can cope with it. She asks me what will happen, how will he be affected by moving? She says that she thinks about it a lot. The children say to her, "How can he go? We are his people."

Nadira tells me that she doesn't call herself "mummy" to him because it would be confusing for him. There is only one mother; he will have another, the adoptive mother; she is only looking after him for now. I say that this time with her, in this family, the love and care she gives him will always be inside him.

As Rahan wakes up, she kisses him. He takes hold of her polo neck and keeps hold of it as she leans back slowly. She comments that he is holding on tight. Observation 6 (4 months, 2 weeks)

It takes time for Nadira to take in the full reality of being a foster parent. Gradually, as she assimilates this reality, she also becomes more able to link the parenting she gives Rahan with the parenting that she has given her own children.

Nadira carries on talking to Rahan as she leaves the room. He mouths the corner of the square toy that she had given him and looks steadily in front of him. When she comes back, I say something about how he watches her when she is there, and, when she leaves, he listens to her voice.

She tells me that she has only just remembered to play peekaboo with him, although she did this with all her children when they were babies. Somehow she'd forgotten about it. She says it helps babies to be able to wait for a bit. Observation 6 (4 months, 2 weeks)

Perhaps for Nadira, overshadowed and preoccupied by the permanent separation that is to come, the game of peekaboo, with its repeated rehearsal of separation and reunion, has felt too raw. Entering a state of mind in which she can play peekaboo with him, recognizing that it helps him, she holds in mind his current development as well as the future separation between them.

Nadira often points out to me that Rahan is dominated by his left side. It comes as a relief when, after weeks of trying to roll over and getting stuck, he finally succeeds in rolling over on both sides.

Rahan tries again and again to roll over, getting stuck each time on his left side. He pulls at the cloth under him to get leverage, but only succeeds in turning himself round. Nadira comments how much he is still dominated by his left side. Rahan's right hand opens and closes repeatedly, in a clutching, almost convulsive movement. Watching this, I feel sad and apprehensive. Observation 8 (5 months)

In my mind, each stage in Rahan's development takes shape alongside the memory of the loss of his birth mother and anticipation of the loss of his foster mother. Watching the clutching movements of his hands I am filled with questions about where he can find a grip and who he can hold on to. I wonder with my supervisor whether, as Rahan internalizes his foster mother, a body memory of the sudden and total loss of his birth mother is reawakened and accentuates his clutching to keep hold.

When the possibility is raised by social workers of Rahan seeing his mother, he turns away from something he sees in my face as Nadira and I talk over what this might be like for him.

Nadira tells me about a phone call from the social work student, telling her she has to take Rahan to meet his birth mother for a "goodbye contact" at the weekend. Nadira is not sure whether she will meet the birth mother or if she is expected to be present during their meeting . . . she ponders what will it be like for him to see his mother? "Will he know her? Of course he will; in his soul he will know."

When Nadira goes into the kitchen, he follows her with his eyes and ears. He gazes at me for a while. As I think about him maybe seeing his birth mother on Saturday, his face suddenly changes, he twists away, reddens, and cries loudly. Observation 10 (5 months, 2 weeks)

In the end, the meeting with his mother does not take place. Against this backdrop of anxiety and uncertainty, Rahan becomes more integrated, in body and in mind.

Rahan lies on his back, draws up his knees, and takes hold of his feet, one in each hand. Then he drops the left foot, almost cries, and then takes both feet in his hands again. He repeats this movement several times. He murmurs and makes repetitive humming sounds.

His stare moves from my face to my feet. When I move my feet, he looks fascinated, then slowly moves his own feet. Observation 10 (5 months, 2 weeks)

While he drops and picks up his left foot, alternating with picking up both feet, Rahan provides himself with a background continuity through the humming sounds that bring together the lips and the front and back of the mouth. As he becomes more linked up with himself, he is then able to link up with me, making full, active eye contact and becoming curious about me and my feet, and about what he can do with his own feet.

I feel pulled between delight in the progress of Rahan's development and the temporary nature of his relationships, which quickly becomes uppermost in my mind:

> Nadira points out to me how Rahan now sits sturdily and confidently upright. She places a basket of toys in front of him and tells me now he can choose and take out the toys himself. But, as we watch, he does not reach into the basket; instead, he pulls up the bedcover underneath the basket so that everything lifts off and the toys all spill out. He does this several times. The thought of the wrench of his having to leave her keeps coming into my mind. I feel a sense of dread. Observation 11 (5 months, 3 weeks)

### A time of limbo

At six months, Rahan is sturdy, compact, and tall for his age. He has wavy ginger-brown hair, his skin is pale, apart from his ruddy cheeks, and his blue-grey eyes are edged with dark lashes. His features are regular, and he often looks as if he is about to laugh, as if expecting a game with the children.

A feeling of merged identities, like a hibernation, once again comes to the fore.

> When the children go back to school, there is a reprise of the merging dynamic between Nadira and Rahan like after the last school holiday. Rahan is unwell again, and Nadira too is in pyjamas. Night and day seem blurred, Nadira and Rahan seem merged; she tells me she was up all night with him—she takes him into the bed next to her so he does not wake the children. Observation 14 (6 months, 2 weeks)

Nadira is now able to hold in mind his prospective adoptive parents as well as his birth mother.

> Nadira turns away after trying to show me Rahan's first tooth, which he covers with his tongue. He watches her and slowly drops the toys from

the high-chair table. He goes on holding the long yellow hair of Dina's little doll. . . .

Changing his nappy, she cleans him deftly, holding both feet in one hand. He smiles up at her and then at me; he seems much more alert and connected now. When she lets go of his feet, he kicks his legs and rolls to one side, then the other. Nadira points out to me how good tempered he is; I reply how well they know each other, how he knows what to expect. She thinks aloud about how much the new parents will have to learn, how much they will need to know about him, and how difficult it will be if they come in the mornings, when there is so much going on here and there are so many comings and goings. . . . She says she will do like me, observe them to see what they understand and what they need to know. Observation 14 (6 months, 2 weeks)

When Rahan is seven months old, we review the observation as planned, and the foster family and social workers agree to continue. There is an expectation that Rahan will move during the next three months, which seems to mitigate the idea that "he could go at any time".

A rather depressed atmosphere sets in. Rahan has a series of colds and minor infections that disturb his sleep. Nadira is often in pyjamas during the observations. Rahan takes to playing with a tattered, collapsed balloon that he bites repeatedly, while I fear it will burst in his face.

Rahan holds the big plastic cricket bat and another toy, and taps the bat on a third toy . . . later on he holds a soft ball and a concave lid that fits around it . . . he struggles to reach another toy and gets stuck, flat on the floor. He struggles to sit up, Nadira encourages him with her voice, and he succeeds in sitting up and smiles widely.

When Nadira goes into the kitchen, Rahan follows her with his eyes and ears. Then he gazes at me for a while. Nadira gives him a floppy balloon, which he clutches. She says she should get him some new toys, he is too old for soft toys now.

. . . He repeats the clutching movement when he is feeding, his hand slowly opening and closing, until she holds him to her and he leans into her between her breasts and puts his hand on her breast and then he is still.

Rahan holds three toys between his hands. One is a little doll with waist-length hair like Nadira's and Dina's. Nadira tells me she held him in her lap all morning before I came. She says she thinks he feels better when I come. I say her lap is a good place for him. Observation 16 (7 months)

The three of us, Nadira, Rahan, and I, have found a way to be together, and he can now hold on to three toys. The ease we have found in being together feels encouraging for the prospect of introducing another "third"—the adoptive parents. But at a time when every knock at the door startles both Nadira and me with the fantasy that someone has come to take the baby away, this triangulated state of mind is fragile: another aspect of "three" feels too much.

> Nadira sings to Rahan, "One, two, buckle my shoe . . ." Observation
> 21 (8 months, 3 weeks)

Nadira breaks off the song: the next line—"three, four, who's at the door?"—feels like a stage too far. Mourning for the tiny baby who is growing up is accompanied by dread of the separation to come. I experience the states of quasi-hibernation into which Nadira and Rahan periodically retreat as, in part, withdrawals from the "too-much-ness" of this experience. The distress and disarray are mitigated by the relief and gratification of seeing Rahan's strength and zest for life, but can only be taken in small doses.

I suggest to Nadira that I could continue to visit her for a few weeks after Rahan goes to the adoptive family, whenever that may be, for us to go on thinking about him and remembering him together. Nadira seems pleased by this idea. She lets me know that my visits help her to feel close to Rahan. However, Nadira's supervising social worker tells me it will not be possible to continue my visits; she thinks Nadira will have another baby placed with her in a matter of days.

## "It is happening now"

The plans for Rahan's move to adoption threaten to repeat something of the unprotected and unmediated journey from the hospital of foster mother and baby.

> Nadira tells me she had "a bad feeling in my heart" when a photographer telephones to say he is coming to take photographs of Rahan to "advertise" him. She says, "What a word for a baby. He is a person, not a thing." Observation 21 (8 months, 3 weeks)

Rahan is nine months old when two prospective adoptive families are mentioned to the foster family. There is a feeling of disarray. When Nadira feeds Rahan, it is too fast, and he vomits.

I follow Kemal, then stop halfway up the stairs when I see that the curtains are drawn in the bedroom and I hear Daamin and Nadira talking quietly. I say hello, and Nadira comes out of the bedroom with Rahan. She sits down on the landing and tells me about the possible adoptive families she has been told about. I don't know where to put myself as I stand halfway up the stairs.

Rahan emerges from a drowsy, dazed-looking state and begins to play peekaboo with me; we peer at each other between the banisters. After a while, Nadira takes Rahan into her lap and looks into the mirror at the top of the stairs with him. He peers into the reflection of the two of them together . . .

Later, Nadira feeds him very fast, at the same time giving him a series of small metal objects one after the other: a hand mirror, a timer, a watch, each of which he instantly drops. . . . She gives him some water in a spoon, but he is suddenly in a rage. He throws the timer hard on the floor, coughs, screams, and vomits.

Kemal asks what is wrong. Nadira says Rahan is upset. "There was too much going on." As she soothes him and wipes his face, she murmurs, "It was too fast." Observation 26 (10 months)

An observation is missed at this time; no one is in when I come, and, unusually, Nadira does not return my phone messages. I worry that the observation may end abruptly, just as Nadira is having to live with the idea that she may never see Rahan again. It feels difficult, possibly intrusive, to ring again, but when I do, Nadira is friendly and keen to arrange the next visit. She tells me that there has been a number of meetings and that the previous families have been ruled out and the social workers are looking for new adopters for Rahan.

Having taken weeks to be able to roll and crawl, Rahan is now standing confidently on his sturdy, muscular legs; soon he takes his first steps. Nadira's children tell her he is too old for all-in-ones now. When he is ten months old, she dresses him in little-boy clothes for the first time. He looks comfortable and has more "shape". But Nadira is flustered and panicky after his little jacket is lost in the shopping centre.

Rahan's constant activity and movement as he stands confidently holding onto a stool with one or two hands, leaning away from it to reach for a tea-towel, looking at me and then away, vocalizing and attracting our attention with radiant or teasing smiles, reminds me of the little baby waving his arms and legs with constant changes of expression crossing his face.

I comment to Nadira on all the sounds he is making. She tells me the children teach him new sounds, like "luraluraloo". I remember the fantasy that came into my mind when he started to vocalize, that his first words would be in the language of his birth family.

Rahan is ten months old today. Nadira says she thinks he will have his first birthday with them. As we watch him standing, she reminds me how long he took to crawl, and says that now his standing up seems quite sudden. She says to him, "Jenifer watched you starting to crawl; now she will see you starting to walk". Observation 26 (10 months)

Nadira links up "then" and "now" for Rahan, and she helps him to link with me; meanwhile, I find it difficult to link up with Rahan's social workers at this time. Although I understand that the observation is, in principle, still supported by the social workers, when I phone or email it is hard for me to feel heard. I struggle to find a voice and to work out how or when to link up with the professional team. There have been two changes of social worker, and I'm not sure how much the new workers know about Rahan, or what they understand about my role.

The observation has been arranged to coincide with the Looked-after Child review meeting. Nadira's supervising social worker does not attend, and Rahan's social worker is replaced by a student social worker. It happens that her first name is almost the same as Rahan's. To my surprise, I catch myself hoping this might mean there could be some kind of connection between them. Observation 29 (11 months)

The Independent Reviewing Officer overseeing the review thanks Nadira on behalf of the local authority for the care she has taken of Rahan.

During the discussion about two possible adoptive families, Rahan repeatedly throws himself backwards, landing on the carpet. He does this again and again, half-crying or moaning, and looking around as if to see who will catch him. I am stunned to see this "who will catch me" game played out so deliberately. Observation 29 (11 months)

Repeatedly throwing himself backwards, Rahan seems to play out a preoccupation with what is going on behind his back. The questioning that this conveys to me about who will hold him feels unbearably poignant.

I wonder with my supervisor about his awareness and whether and how something of his provisional position may have been conveyed to Rahan.

As summer arrives, a mediated transition between inside and outside is worked through.

> Rahan stands with Dina looking over the board Nadira has placed to enclose the porch. He looks comfortable and sturdy in blue shorts and T-shirt. He looks into the alleyway in front of the house where the next-door children are running up and down. Nadira tells them not to move the board, otherwise Rahan will go out. Observation 32 (11 months, 3 weeks)

Nadira has created an enclosed, safe transitional space for Rahan in which he can wander freely. But at times I see him roaming from room to room or sitting in a trance-like state, his gaze unfocused.

> Rahan is running up and down in the sitting room. . . . Later, he sits in a trance with a distant expression. I don't manage to make eye contact with him for more than a moment. I have the feeling of not really meeting him or Nadira throughout the observation today. Observation 34 (12 months, 1 week)

Nadira describes the planning meetings that she attends as "very heavy". I hear from Rahan's social worker that "the schedule is too full" to explore the possibility of my meeting the adoptive mother and that it will not be possible for me to continue to observe Rahan in his new home. Nadira expresses her own disappointment about this. She had hoped that Rahan would have the continuity of my visiting him in his new home. She herself has been given no indication as to whether she may see him after he is adopted. I wonder with my supervisor if Rahan's roaming and withdrawal may be his response to a Nadira who is practising in her mind to let him go. When Nadira and her daughter Dina blow bubbles for Rahan to catch, he remains seated and, in a trance, watches them float away in the air. I, too, feel distant: Rahan, Nadira, and the social work team all seem hard to find, and I find myself withdrawing and losing track of time.

> Rahan clings to Nadira's legs. Then she sits on a little stool and takes him on her lap in the hall. She tells me this is a nice cool and airy place while it's so hot outside. Rahan lies comfortably on her lap, her arm firmly around him. She holds him closely; they are both quiet and still.

Dina talks to her mother about Rahan's birthday next week. Rahan slides off Nadira's lap with a new movement that Kemal pointed out to me last week. Rahan goes to watch the children in the alleyway.

Dina blows bubbles and encourages Rahan to try to catch them, but mainly he watches with concentration as they melt away and vanish. Nadira blows some bubbles inside the hall where they are easier for him to catch. He looks at me in a wondering way. I feel we are all very much engaged in thinking about Rahan's imminent disappearance.

In the kitchen, Nadira washes his feet, then his face with water from the palm of her hand. She smooths his hair back. He looks more boyish and older with his hair flat. He follows the movements of her hand, and rubs his own face. He looks refreshed. He smiles widely when I say it looks nice and cool. Nadira offers him first a bottle of milk then a bottle of water—he takes one suck of each, then pushes it resolutely away.

A little later, he slides on to his bottom and sits on the floor collapsed against a cupboard. Nadira takes him into the bedroom upstairs where the curtains are drawn against the hot sun. She puts him in the cot where the children take it in turns to play with him. Dina climbs into the cot and plays "This little piggy" with him.

Rahan grabs Kemal's hair and pulls hard. Kemal winces but submits with a smile. Nadira tells me he was doing this today in the crèche with the other children. He leans out of the cot and pushes the alarm clock off the side of the bedside table. Dina complains to her mother that he may break it. Nadira tells her it is an old clock that all the children played with when they were little; she doesn't think it's going to break now. Observation 32 (11 months, 3 weeks)

The last observations before Rahan meets his adoptive mother are hard for me to think about and remember. We are faced with the prospect that Rahan's leaving will be as unmediated as his arrival in the foster family. Months before, when it became possible for Nadira to play peekaboo with Rahan, it seemed that this may have helped her to take in and accept something of the reality that his coming to the family would be followed by his leaving. Now, with a sombre sense of this reality being so imminent, it was as if both foster mother and child were able to take refuge in a regulated retreat that left each of them still available for moments of close intimacy.

Rahan is fast asleep on his back with his face turned towards the duck toy and with one hand resting on it. He is completely still, and his breathing is silent. Nadira comes up to check on him and tells me while he sleeps about the cooking she is doing with her seventeen-year-old niece. Rahan stirs and twists in his sleep but does not wake up. He takes his left thumb into his mouth.

When Nadira leaves the room, his hands move slowly and the fingers of his left hand fan out, open and close again. Slowly his thumb drops out of his mouth; there is no check in his breathing. He slightly opens and closes his right hand, then his left. This reminds me of the clenching and unclenching he was doing a few months ago.

As he sleeps, Nadira wonders how he will manage in a quiet house after being here with all the children. She says, "Part of our heart is ripped—goes away with him. We will all miss him, I will miss him." I hear a knock at the door, and immediately I brace myself, thinking it is someone coming to take him away right now.

Nadira says she will take a photo of me to put in his book, and they will take my birthday present with him when they go. She says he will need to know who Jenifer is, who came to see him every Thursday.

Rahan turns his head away when I say goodbye and stares at me blankly as I leave. Observation 33 (12 months)

In the following observation, Salim—Nadira and Daamin's oldest son —patiently assembles a tricycle out of many different parts. I notice that I feel intensely curious about the packing boxes in the hall, intensely disappointed not to see the present I gave to Nadira for him, and intensely impatient for the tricycle to be assembled,

Rahan is running up and down in the sitting room. At one point he comes towards me pointing a pink fluffy wand, then he veers away and runs past me.

When Nadira lifts Rahan onto the seat of the tricycle, he sits in a bit of a trance with a distant expression. His feet don't reach the pedals, and when she lifts him off after a moment, he sobs and screams desperately. Nadira comforts him, holding him close. She shows him a tiny leaf, then finds another one, and shows him how he can put them into the little basket that hangs behind the seat of the bike. He is very pleased and immediately fascinated and engaged with this.

A little later, Rahan imitates Nadira's posture as she leans her back against the brick wall of the alleyway. Then he sets off to walk to the end of the alleyway and the locked gate looking on to the busy road beyond. He watches cars passing with the same almost vacant look. He seems to walk confidently on the paving stones but suddenly he falls quite hard on his face. His nose is bleeding, and Nadira says she can see it hurt. He has a long drink of water, and Nadira takes him upstairs to lie down. Observation 34 (12 months, 1 week)

During the hot summer days of the last observations, I feel I am only now taking in the enormity of the loss imminently facing Rahan. He is often outside with Dina, Kemal, and the neighbours' children for part of my visit, and part of the time inside the house with Nadira.

> Rahan looks towards me with a dreamy expression. Nadira tells me he is very day-dreamy at the moment. She asks him if he is looking at the leaves blowing in the wind. He goes up and down the alleyway with the boys; they kick the ball for him, and he follows it as it rolls. It gets windy. Rahan half closes his eyes as the wind ruffles his hair; he puts his hands over his ears, and rubs his tummy. He says, "Hoarrhhh", making a sound like the wind. He goes in and out of the house many times to see Nadira using the Hoover. When she has finished hoovering, he goes up to the Hoover, which he used to be scared of, touches it and smiles proudly, looking round at us.
>
> Nadira tells him he is brave and praises him. He says in a long, slow exhalation, "Hoooover", and we all comment on his word. She gives him a cup of water; he drinks deeply, then holds the cup out to me.
>
> Thinking about this move and what it will be like for Rahan, Nadira reflects that, later on, Rahan will think about his birth mother and father, but that will be when he is older. Right now, she is like the mother: for him, at the moment, it is about her and the adoptive mother. She says, "All that time we were thinking about it and expecting it, and now I am thinking: it is happening now." Observation 35 (12 months, 2 weeks)

In the penultimate observation, Rahan's play has a serious quality, acting out a coming and going that for me seems to reflect the rhythm of my comings and goings in the foster home. His play also seems to express a capacity to fluctuate between being more or less integrated, more or less connected, that I feel may help to sustain him during the separation from Nadira and the beginning of his new life with his adoptive mother.

> Rahan plays a slow game of peekaboo with me, which feels serious and enquiring. He brings the duck toy to me, watching me carefully, and gives it to me and takes it back many times. Then he throws it down on the floor, picks it up, and holds it close, embracing it in both arms and burrowing his face into it. Observation 36 (12 months, 3 weeks)

After this visit, I learn that the time for Rahan and his adoptive mother to be introduced and for her to spend time with him in the foster home has been reduced to four days and that the plan is for the adoptive mother to travel alone with Rahan to her home. This is because no social worker was available to accompany them on the agreed date. Nadira tells me she offered to go with them, perhaps with her seventeen-year-old niece who also knew Rahan well, but had been told that this would not be allowed. I take an opportunity to reflect with social work managers on my observations of the closeness between Rahan and his foster mother and his acute sensitivity to abrupt separations. Now thirteen months old, he is sturdy, rosy-cheeked, and lively, but I also have in mind a Rahan who can become unreachable and profoundly distressed when not held together in his foster mother's attention. The observational, lived experience that I am able to draw on communicates something that convinces his social workers of Rahan's need for a more integrated transition and more continuity between his foster and adoptive homes. Nadira is asked to accompany him on the day of his move and to be there to help him settle the following day.

> It is a hot, sunny day. Rahan looks comfortable in a nappy and a T-shirt. He points to the shoes in the hall and says "shoes". He plays with a long wooden stick with a red ball on the end, which he uses to point and to touch things. Then he stands whimpering by Nadira, who is sitting with Dina in her lap. Nadira tells her to get down and takes Rahan into her lap. He nestles and moulds into her body. She feeds him strawberries; he glows with delight and looks into her face, and she kisses him.
>
> Dina and Nadira take photos of Rahan on my lap, using Salim's phone. They play a song on the phone that they tell me is his favourite. He sits in my lap and listens to the song several times over.
>
> Later he plays in the alleyway with the boys. He falls over several times, tripping over the ends of his soft shoes. Each time he supports himself firmly on his hands and forearms, keeping his head up, cushioning his fall. The boys comment that he knows how to fall without getting hurt. Observation 37 (13 months)

## Afterwards

In my first visit to Nadira after Rahan moves, she and her daughter Dina each tell me their dreams about Rahan. Nadira tells me how hard she tried to connect with the adoptive mother, to help Rahan feel safe with her. Dina shows me a mobile she made for Rahan. It has a different symbol for each member of the foster family, and a sun and moon in the middle for Rahan and the adoptive mother.

Two and a half months later, I hear that the adoptive family have invited the foster family to visit Rahan in his new home. Nadira does not know whether they will see him again after this, but when I meet her again four months later, I am relieved and heartened to hear about a growing closeness that has developed between the adoptive and foster families.

# CHAPTER FOUR

# Learning from the research

The single-case study that I was able to carry out with Rahan, his foster family, and his social workers showed that it was possible to conduct a therapeutic observation with a baby and his foster carer until he was moved to adoption. The weekly observation visits were accepted by the foster family and the social work network. The foster carer welcomed me into her home, shared her own observations with me, and kept me informed of developments. She let me know that my regular visits helped her to feel close to her foster child and supported her in her role as foster carer, and I was able to remain in contact with her after Rahan moved. The weekly observational visits allowed me to experience something of the intensity of the shared journey of foster mother and child and to take in something of the disturbance that accompanies each developmental advance when a permanent separation is anticipated.

The research yielded many areas for learning. The disappointing result that it did not prove possible for me to meet the adoptive family or to continue to observe Rahan in his new home highlighted the need for the clinician and the clinical team to be proactive from the outset in advocating for as much continuity as possible for young children moving to adoption. Although communication with the social work network fluctuated, I was able to draw on the observations to contribute to planning for the move to adoption. The local authority fostering

service and the social work teams were open to discussing how findings from the study could inform practice and training. After the
research was disseminated, there was an increase in referrals for support for babies and young children and their foster carers and requests
for training in relation to the needs of babies and young children in
care.

Rahan's circumstances were unusual in that there were no care proceedings, he had no placement moves before his move to adoption,
and there was no contact with his birth family. Although this made his
situation very different from that of most infants in care, carrying out
this research gave me a deeper understanding of universal elements of
the experience of babies in transition. I became more aware of the tremendous impact of transitions and changes at the very beginning of
life; of the emotional endurance of the foster carer and the foster
family, providing a home in their hearts and minds for the growing
infant while living with the knowledge that he will go and uncertainty
about whether they will ever see him again; and of the foster carer's
exquisitely complex task of acting as a bridge between birth and adoptive parents, always judging how much to reach out and how much to
stand back.

I learned more, too, about what it can be like to experience the "cor-
porate parenting" that is provided for children in care. Rahan and
Nadira were thrown together by the circumstances in which he was
brought from the hospital, and it seemed that this was immediately followed by an idea of tearing them apart with the message, *"remember he
is not yours"*. The suddenness of Rahan's arrival reverberated in the
foster mother's mind and seemed to be amplified by the idea that *"he
could go at any time"*. The risk of the move to adoption repeating the
sudden and unmediated transition from his birth mother to his foster
mother may also have reflected the impact of troubled relationships in
his birth family where intimacy was linked with the risk of violence.
Anxieties about his mother's safety may have made it harder to sustain
a focus on Rahan's experiences and needs and contributed to the
length of time it took to identify an adoptive family for him.

## Understanding more about transitions

After a long period of uncertainty for the foster family, and periods
when time seemed to be on hold, as soon as a decision was made
about Rahan's adoption things seemed to move very fast. The shorten-
ing of the introduction period is consistent with the studies of moves

from foster care to adoption discussed in chapter 1, which have shown that excitement, anxiety, and hopefulness about the child's new life can tend to blot out the significance of the child's relationships with foster carers. Nadira and the foster family had to address within themselves the uncertainties of not knowing how best to help Rahan with the separation from them, not knowing how it would affect them, and not knowing whether they could continue to have a relationship with him. The emotional work of foster caring also included the provision of a "family envelope" for Rahan that would protect and buffer him from exposure to the fate of a lost or unwanted child. Nadira was able to take on the task of mediating the rupture of the link with his birth mother and the move to his adoptive family so that he could take in something more joined up.

There were several changes of social worker for Rahan. In my role as the observer, I noticed that it felt more difficult for me to maintain communication with the social work network each time a new social worker was allocated. The experiential knowledge from the observation motivated me to persist in reaching out to the network and to go on linking with them: I had heard from Nadira and seen and felt for myself how different things were for Rahan when the adults around him were able to come together. I could speak from experience about how much a more contained and cohesive professional network helped him to connect with his carer and to become more connected within himself. These were important findings for his development that the social work professionals were able to take into account in the planning of the move to adoption.

The observation provided many opportunities to see how significant play and playfulness could be for a baby in transition, mediating the impact of disruptions and affording moments of shared delight and reprieve for Rahan and his foster family. The role of therapeutic observer also involved taking in and absorbing painful feelings of dread and grief when the provisional nature of the foster carer–child relationship seemed to impact on the capacity for play. This emotional communication with the observer at times seemed to release something for Nadira and Rahan that helped to facilitate play. An important change came when Nadira became able to play peekaboo with Rahan. As she recognized, peekaboo allows experiences of separation to be experimented with and explored, giving the infant a degree of agency and helping to develop the capacity to anticipate and manage a separation. This was a moment during the observation that alerted me to ways in which aspects of ordinary parenting may be subtly inhibited in a temporary foster-caring relationship.

In the penultimate observation, Rahan's play had a profoundly serious quality. With the duck toy he had been given when he was four
months old, he acted out a coming and going that seemed to reflect the
rhythm of my comings and goings in the foster home. For me, knowing that I would not see him again after the final observation visit, this
deeply felt play seemed to demonstrate his ability to remember and to
symbolize. I felt encouraged by witnessing these capacities that I
thought might help him during the separation from Nadira and the
beginning of his new life with his adoptive mother.

## The therapeutic observer's role

An important aspect of my role was to be a companion on the journey
with Nadira and Rahan. As Rhode (2007) highlights, the therapeutic
observer's tasks include receiving and absorbing impressions, spanning
from fleeting, momentary sensations to grosser shocks. Events, feelings,
and thoughts that had not yet fully become conscious were experienced
during the observation hour as raw and intense. I came to see parallels
between these powerful experiences and the experiences that have
been reported in the studies of premature babies described in chapter 1.
I felt guilt when Rahan, at his most isolated and lost, came across to
me as ugly. There were times when I wanted to get away; at other
times, I felt an unspoken pressure not to look. As I witnessed the growing closeness between Rahan and his foster mother, and as I found a
place for myself with them as someone who could emotionally know
and understand something of their experience, he became a beautiful
baby and the relationship between him and Nadira became beautiful to
witness.

Rhode also discusses another way in which the observer gains an
experiential understanding of the family context in which the child
grows up, by identifying in turn with different members of the family
as well as with the observed child. The therapeutic observer of a child
in care has repeated opportunities to identify with the members of the
foster family and with social workers as well as with the child who is
the subject of the observation. My experience as the planning for
Rahan's adoption took shape of finding it hard even to find a voice
may reflect my identification with the foster carers who parented
Rahan but had no voice in the decisions about his future. It may also
reflect my identification with Rahan, whose need for continuity and
whose attachment to his primary carers seemed to be swept out of
mind as the adoption came closer. At the same time, I was mindful of

the social workers' concerns and the anxieties they had been left with. Voicing my thoughts and feelings during the last stage of Rahan's foster placement meant that, as part of my role as therapeutic observer, I was advocating for the parenting he had received in his foster home and for the "going-on linking" that I had seen to be crucial in his development. The detail that I was able to bring from the observations seemed to enhance a focus on Rahan's states of mind and his needs, despite the potential clash between strongly held views from different professional perspectives about different ways of managing the move to adoption. The observational perspective helped to bring a shift from the idea of a "clean break" to the idea that, in moving on, Rahan would be most supported by the adults being able to link up around him. This was consistent with the finding reported in chapter 1 from therapeutic observations in medical contexts that a focus on the baby's experience can help to find ways of working that are acceptable to parents and professionals.

## Themes

The grounded theory method I used to analyse the observation notes involves a line-by-line analysis that fits well with the detailed note-writing of the therapeutic observation model. Although I tried to put a theoretical perspective to one side when I analysed the data, the themes that I identified reflected central areas in research and clinical thinking about children in care. The fragmenting impact of disrupted attachments discussed in chapter 1 was a central theme throughout the observation (Wakelyn, 2011).

"Coming together and apart" became apparent as a central theme in the first stage of the data analysis. When I examined the material further, I was able to identify four distinct ways of coming together and apart which I had observed between Rahan and Nadira and in the dynamics of the professional network. I also recognized these ways of functioning at different times in my own emotional responses. The four ways of coming together and apart seemed to represent distinct modes of functioning. I chose these metaphors to name them: Matrix, Tornado, Machine, and Limbo.

### Matrix

My first visit brought a powerful example of the theme of coming together, when my impressions of Rahan as a lost baby who had somehow remained distant changed as Nadira reflected aloud on their first coming together. As they then seemed to find each other, Rahan himself became more gathered together and joined up. This is an example of Matrix functioning: a regulated way of coming together that seems to help people to feel connected and contained and allows feelings to be linked with thoughts even when they are painful, sad, or unexpected. I had been moved by how Rahan's social worker had held in mind a constellation of relationships that were important for Rahan that seemed to maintain the idea of a meaningful connection with his birth mother after they had parted. It was striking, too, that the social work team was able to come together to support the continuity of relationships for the thirteen-month-old Rahan when the time came for him to move to a new family. Another aspect of Matrix functioning, which came and went during the observations, could be seen in my fluctuating capacity to think and to make connections in my mind between present, past, and future. As a further example, Rahan's play in the penultimate observational visit seemed to combine a deep seriousness with playfulness. The capacities to remember and to symbolize that this play seemed to evince are aspects of the internal continuity discussed in chapter 1 as a protective factor for children experiencing external discontinuities.

The research suggested that Matrix dynamics helped the foster mother and baby to attune to each other and, at the same time, supported working-group dynamics in the professional team that could focus on Rahan's needs (Bion, 1961, 1970). Matrix functioning involves integration, taking in from the external environment to feed inner life and the personality. As a state of mind in which learning and development are possible, Matrix also encompasses the endeavour of the research project to learn from experience and to promote the development of professionals through their work.

## Tornado

The metaphor of "Tornado" denotes overwhelming experiences of feeling under pressure and fragmented. When coming together and apart happens in this way, feelings are raw and extreme. In this mode of functioning, fragmented and dysregulated states of mind impede contact with the emotional reality of the child.

Rahan's unmediated coming together with his foster carer at the door of the hospital is an example of Tornado functioning. This event seemed to echo and repeat something that had been undigested and frightening for the social workers and nurses in the hospital about the concealed pregnancy and the sudden loss of his mother on the day of his birth.

This mode of functioning is akin to shock. There is little sense of time or sequence; separations and reunions are sudden, unprepared, and unpredictable. It feels difficult to bring thoughts and feelings together. After the first observations, it was striking that the impact of what felt like fragmented bits of experience that it was hard to bring together left me feeling drained and exhausted.

## Machine

The Machine mode of coming together and apart is characterized by dissociation. Contact with emotional reality is lost as the result of thoughts being cut off from feelings. We all need to cut off to some degree some of the time; in work with children in care, the pain of loss and breakdown is too much for one person to hold in mind all the time. But rather than a regulatory withdrawal and the recognition that there are others who can share the task that would be present in Matrix functioning, Machine states of mind represent the extreme of cynical, mechanical thinking with no human core. The impact of loss is dismissed; people are treated as things, and one person is seen as interchangeable with another. Imaginative empathy is hard to summon up in this atmosphere.

Suzanne Maiello (2007) describes an aim of observational interventions as promoting the integration of paternal and maternal aspects of the container. In Machine functioning, a profound split between paternal and maternal aspects of parenting was apparent in the divide between the social workers and foster carers. Decision making, an aspect of paternal function, was located in social workers, while the maternal functions of attention, receptivity, and emotionality were located in the foster carers. The position of the foster carers was of the greatest emotional connectedness to Rahan and the least agency and power to make decisions about him. The foster carers had to accept their relegation to a role largely without agency or decision-making power. As an experienced mother of three children, Nadira was instructed in how to bath Rahan, when to take him to playgroup, and what toys were safe for him and was not allowed to take him on a family holiday.

Machine modes of functioning seemed particularly powerful as the time came for the move to adoption, with the idea that Rahan would quickly forget his foster family and that Nadira could be distracted with a new baby to look after. The denial of loss and of the significance of the individuality and uniqueness of intimate relationships seemed to bring pervasive feelings of bleakness and depression.

## Limbo

In the fourth mode of coming together and apart, Limbo, development is on hold because relationships and circumstances go on being provisional and temporary for too long. The temporary nature of parenting in the foster home seemed to be linked to the developmental game of peekaboo dropping out of mind. The Limbo state was particularly marked in the middle period of the observation. While the search for an adoptive family went on, ordinary life seemed to be on hold for the foster family. Reality seemed to be suspended and held at bay:

> Night and day seem blurred; Nadira and Rahan seem merged . . .

In Limbo, loss of contact with emotional reality occurs through a form of suspended animation that blurs the rhythm of development, merges past, present, and future, and brings the pervasive feelings of unreality that Philps (2003) describes as a feature of borderline psychopathology.

## The dynamics of trauma

Tornado, Machine, and Limbo each represent aspects of the fragmenting, isolating, and deadening experience of trauma. They afford some protection from overwhelming stress, but at the cost of contact with the emotional reality of the child and with the most sensitive parts of the self. My research suggested that when these ways of functioning combine, organization is more likely to be driven by the dynamics of trauma. A sign of this would be vicious circles of mis-attunement and disassociation that create escalating distress and confusion.

My experience of therapeutic observation was that it has the potential to intervene in this dynamic through a focus on the individual child's emotional experiences and needs. This way of working also highlights the crucial significance of close relationships with caregivers, which cannot be given up without feelings of mourning and loss. When adults are able to come together to hold the child's emotional reality in mind, the collective containment of Matrix functioning allows these feelings to be regulated and mitigates the impact of loss and disruption for the child.

## Dissemination and service development

When the research findings were disseminated through feedback meetings, workshops, and conversations with social workers, the service began to receive more referrals for babies and young children in care. Social workers began to consult with clinicians more frequently during family finding and when planning placement moves for babies and young children. Training workshops with a focus on exploring and learning from the experiences of all those involved in transitions for young children have provided opportunities to continue to learn from each other and to build up shared knowledge and understanding of the experiences of the youngest children in care.

# CHAPTER FIVE

# Therapeutic observation in clinical practice

As clinicians in a mental health service for children in care, we have found therapeutic observation a helpful intervention with infants and young children in foster care, particularly when there are concerns about the impact of early trauma, compromised development, or an impending transition. A central aim of these interventions is to get to know the child better and to understand more about what may be stressful for him or her and what forms of support are most likely to be helpful. There may also be more specific aims, such as promoting closer attunement between foster carer and child, or gaining a better understanding of a developmental delay or of emotional or behavioural difficulties. In addition to the observational visits, the interventions also involve regular meetings with professional networks and contributing to care planning.

Therapeutic observation interventions are often open-ended: those described in this chapter range in duration from four months to two years. The approach is flexible in relation to the frequency of visits, while adhering to the fundamental requirement of a regular observation time, detailed recording after the visit, and regular supervision for the clinician. The frequency of observational visits will reflect the acuteness of concerns or the timescale of an imminent move and may also depend on the foster carer's commitments and the resources available. Once-weekly observations are often difficult for foster carers to manage if they are also taking children to contact sessions and medical or developmental appointments. A visit every two or three weeks is often more practicable, sometimes with telephone contact with the foster carer between visits. With less frequent visiting, there is, of course, more difficulty in maintaining a sense of continuity.

## The clinician's role

Prior training in psychoanalytic infant observation equips clinicians to take on the role of therapeutic observer. The role requires mental energy and commitment from the clinician as well as time for travelling to the foster home and detailed note-writing after each visit. Consistency and reliability are also essential prerequisites of therapeutic observation. Clinicians need to be prepared to find themselves on the receiving end of powerful projections from the child, the foster carer, and the professional network; they need also to be robust and committed to withstanding these projections with the support of supervision. The supervisor should be an experienced clinician. The containment and understanding in supervision aims to help clinicians to remain receptive, open-minded, and curious, noticing the pressures and demands of the role and exploring their emotional responses to the observed interactions.

Rooted in the close detail of child development and the experiential understanding of the transitions and disruptions that are a feature of life in care, therapeutic observation provides a rich learning experience that can be invaluable for clinical work with children of all ages. It may be difficult in the present climate to make the case for longer term or open-ended interventions. In the cases described in this chapter, the interventions have been provided as part of the continuing professional development required for all mental health professionals. Managers may also be mindful of the value for a multidisciplinary team of learning from ongoing work that brings a close connection with the unfolding relationships between foster carer and child early in life. For mental health teams often responding to acute situations and emergencies, the focus in observational work on a slow unravelling and the moment-to-moment significance of interactions can bring valuable reminders both of the ongoing reverberations of trauma and of the strength of the life-seeking drive for development. This focus can be particularly helpful for teams working "beyond the family envelope" where the basic principles of responsiveness and continuity repeatedly need to be rediscovered. Reflecting on the earliest and formative stages of an infant's life has also helped clinicians to be alert to the impact of transitions for older children and adolescents.

## Setting up a therapeutic observation

The support of a clinical team and regular supervision are prerequisites in the setting for work that brings clinicians close to the experiences of young children in care in ways that can be both distressing and rewarding. At the outset, clinician and supervisor should agree the remit of their roles: the clinician may take on the role of communicating with and feeding back to the professional network, or in some situations it may be more appropriate for the supervisor to take on this aspect of the work. As a first stage, it is helpful to set up a meeting with the foster carer, the supervising social worker, and the child's social worker and other professionals who are currently involved. This provides an opportunity to explore what the observation involves and why it is being offered and to agree a review process and lines of communication. Ideas about how best to prepare for a transition when a permanent placement is identified can also be shared in an introductory meeting. Drawing on the research outlined in chapter 1, unless there are particular logistic or other complexities, we recommend visits to the child by the foster carers soon after the move. For many children and their new families, continuing the connection with previous foster carers can also be beneficial (Schofield, 2018).

In this chapter, I describe two therapeutic observations carried out by clinicians in a specialist mental health service for children in care which I had the opportunity to supervise. In the last section, recurrent themes in therapeutic observation are explored.

## Ania

Therapeutic observation was offered to provide a closer acquaintance with Ania, a baby born prematurely who was taken into care at birth. This intervention went on to last for two years. The clinician, Martina Weilandt, is an experienced clinical social worker and mental health practitioner whose training included psychoanalytic infant observation.

Ania's parents suffered from severe mental health and substance-abuse difficulties, which led to the decision for Ania to be placed in care from birth. Three children had been removed from her mother in the previous eight years. Ania was born four weeks premature with foetal distress after her mother had taken a high dose of heroin. She had also been exposed to cocaine *in utero*. Ania's neonatal withdrawal symptoms required treatment with morphine in the hospital's special care baby unit. A heart murmur was also detected, which needed continuing follow up. In the neonatal unit, Ania received specialist care for three weeks from the rota of nurses working in the ward.

One of the effects of foetal exposure to drugs and the subsequent withdrawal can be prolonged crying that has a very piercing quality. The babies are difficult to comfort and may need to be held, carried, and soothed for hours on end. Ania's first foster carer, who was also looking after two young children, found Ania's inconsolable distress more than she could manage. After three months this placement came to an end. Ania now faced a further separation and a move away from the familiar voices, smells, and routines of the first foster home. She was taken to Sharon, an experienced foster carer who, with no other children in her care and with the support of her adult daughter, was able to provide Ania with her undivided attention for much of the day.

When Ania first came to her, Sharon reported that it was difficult to understand what she wanted or needed; withdrawn states alternated with shrill, inconsolable crying. She needed constant attention, and caring for her was demanding. It took a lot of patience to encourage her to drink from her bottle. She was difficult to settle or soothe, waking up frequently during the night. Ania seemed stiff in her upper body, particularly in one arm. Ania's social worker gave a vivid description of her when she was three months old:

> A tiny baby with rigid muscle tone, tense, stiff, lying curved like a ball just beginning to straighten and relax. She was screaming in a high-pitched tone that would go on and on until she would suddenly stop. It felt nothing could be done to help this.

In a consultation with the social worker and foster carer, an open-ended observational intervention was agreed while care proceedings were carried out to establish Ania's future care. It was agreed that fortnightly visits to the foster placement would be combined with regular meetings with the professional network and that the observer would meet her future caregivers when her placement had been agreed.

In her first visit, Martina's impressions of Ania, now four months old, were of an infant who seemed very far away:

> Ania seemed rather pale and stiff. . . . When Sharon left the room, Ania did not look at me. I felt very uncomfortable with the situation of being

alone with her. The silence and aloneness after a time seemed too long, and I moved to sit nearer, and talked to her quietly. Ania stretched up her left arm until it was rigid, making her hand into a fist. She remained in this tense position until Sharon returned.

In her second visit, Martina was again left alone with Ania for a few minutes. This time, Ania made a tentative movement towards the observer:

> Ania stared at me with blank eyes for what felt a very long time. Then she slowly moved her arm and placed her hand on my wrist. I was taken aback by Ania's deliberate movement and by the lightness of her touch, like a feather, as if I had to hold my breath in not to blow her away. Ania looked into my face, her eyes brighter. I stayed very still and talked quietly to Ania until Sharon returned.

In these first visits, Martina saw a baby with whom it was difficult to connect. Ania seemed to actively block Martina out from her perceptions, turning her face away from her and not reacting when Martina talked to her. She had a serious facial expression that rarely changed. Martina learned that making contact with Ania had to be slow and gradual: a movement that was too quick or a sound that was too loud could make her instantly withdraw. Yet once it was established, the contact between Martina and the 3-month-old baby felt very intense. Over time, Martina noticed a similar pattern in her interactions with Sharon. Many of her visits were cancelled or postponed; sometimes Martina waited several minutes after ringing at the door, leaving her wondering if her visit had been forgotten or was not wanted. But once she had been let in, Martina was warmly welcomed and left in no doubt that she was expected. It was as if a protective layer that encircled the foster carer-and-baby couple required particular persistence to get through.

Martina observed Ania making slow but steady progress in the warm, attentive, and thoughtful care of Sharon and her family. It took time for Sharon to get to know Ania and find the right approaches for her. Martina noticed that Ania often became unsettled when she was lying on her back and could not see what other people in the room were doing. She seemed to become more relaxed once she was able to roll over, and then to sit up. Despite at times feeling exhausted, Sharon kept thinking about different ways of understanding and helping Ania—for example, learning to do baby massage with her. When it was found in the statutory health review that Ania was not yet at the stage of pulling a little toy by a string, Sharon bought several of these toys for her so that she would be able to show the paediatrician in the next assessment that she could do it.

Martina had been visiting for two months when Sharon received the shocking news that Ania's mother had died from an overdose. During her next visit, there was a profound sense of contact between Martina and Ania:

> Ania sat in front of me, looking at me seriously. She took hold of my hand and held it. I spoke gently in a quiet voice. As Ania continued to look into my eyes, I responded by stroking her hand. Every now and then Ania made a big sigh, with her shoulders and chest moving. There were long periods when both of us were silent. I felt a deep sense of connectedness with her.

The impact of Ania's mother's death was devastating, fragmenting the cohesion of a previously well-established professional network. Phone calls and emails to professionals went unanswered during this period. Sharon now seemed to be in a vacuum and felt very much the sole carer for Ania. As the closest person to her, Sharon was experiencing pain and grief on Ania's behalf, as well as holding the responsibility of being the closest adult in her life. Martina found that re-establishing communication with the network required persistence. As with her visits to the foster home, once contact had been made it was welcomed. When the meetings resumed, the professionals in the network made it clear that they valued Martina's contributions from the observation and the meetings that she continued to convene.

As the working group of professionals once more began to cohere, Martina noticed a new arrangement of furniture in the living room of the foster home. The sofas and armchairs were arranged in a circle in the middle of the room, with a small table forming a movable doorway into the enclosed and cushioned space within. This seemed both to represent a womb-like space and a protective buffer for Ania against an external world felt to be harsh and dangerous. Perhaps, too, it offered a buffer against a future cruel knowledge for Ania of her mother's death. Here Ania could be kept safe, and the impact of her bereavement could be gradually processed and, some of the time, set aside. As Martina had needed to persist in reaching out to cross the boundary between outside and inside to establish the regular routine of her visits, so now getting inside the circle of couches took an effort; but once inside, the feeling was one of "*now you were in, now we could actually just be"*. The protective zone of the circle of couches seemed to both symbol-ize and concretely provide a place of reprieve from feelings of shock and grief.

Tragically, six weeks later Ania was again bereaved. Her father, too, had died suddenly; the cause of his death remained unclear. The loss of her remaining parent created a profound sense of shock and grief in those around Ania. His parents, who were living in another country, soon decided to put themselves forward to adopt Ania. Remaining within her birth family seemed to offer potential for hope, alongside anx-iety about whether her complex needs could be met by her grandparents, and about the impact of their son's death on the family as a whole. There was prolonged uncertainty as assessments continued for five months, while the potential move to another country threatened an abso-lute severance of the close bond Ania had formed with Sharon. Martina described Sharon's position during this transitional period in this way:

> Living in a "stuck transition" and managing the complexity of caring for a child with an uncertain future, balancing the need to provide a loving home and allowing a close bond to develop, whilst at the same time knowing that she will move on.

## "You have seen it"

When she was upset, tired, or hurt, Ania accepted comfort from Sharon rather reluctantly, but gradually she began to turn to her more. This important development helped Sharon to feel that Ania would be able to make her needs known and find comfort from her future care-givers. After Ania's grandparents were positively assessed, Sharon was keen to get to know and help them, so that she would know who Ania was going to be with, but also so that there would be time for Ania to get to know her grandparents while still being able to turn to her for reassurance and comfort. It was now Sharon who advocated for Marti-na's continuing involvement in the professional network, insisting that she was integral to the planning and should be there when the grand-parents first came to see Ania:

> You have been coming to visit us for such a long time. You have seen it. You are important in Ania's life.

Ania's grandparents had been talking on the phone with Sharon and Skyp-ing for several months before their first visit. A three-week introductory period followed when they visited the foster home every day, learned Ania's routines, and gradually spent more time with her alone. That this introductory period was longer than usual was acknowledged by the professional network to reflect a deeper understanding of Ania's needs as a result of Martina's direct observations. Martina was also able to use her observations to help the adoptive parents imagine what might be involved for Ania in forming new attachments and moving to a new country where even the sound of people's voices and the language she was hearing would be different. She could draw on repeated observations to describe how quickly Ania could be overwhelmed by too many new experiences or new adults too soon. She was able to advocate for Ania's need for a gradual, integrated transition and to think each stage through with her social workers. The network was able to recognize that Ania's traits of premature self-sufficiency meant that she did not seek help easily and might lead to her being thought to be self-reliant, when in fact she needed more attuned care and individual attention than a toddler growing up in more ordinary circumstances.

Ania was two and a quarter years old when she was taken to her new home. We heard that the extended family gathered around, and one of her uncles became an active helper to her grandparents. Her grandparents maintained contact with Sharon, talking with her on Skype, seeking her advice and sending photos. They asked Martina to send a letter that they could use to help find psychological support from services in their country.

## Discussion

A central task throughout this intervention was bringing the professional network together in order to keep Ania in the forefront of the thinking and to reduce potential delays in her permanent placement once it had been decided on. Martina succeeded in maintaining communication with professionals throughout the observation and in linking with Ania's family. Another aspect of Martina's role was to validate Sharon's observations of Ania's development, share her own observations, and describe her understanding of Ania's psychological needs. Staying connected with the reality of Ania's experiences was a key task that seemed to be at once valued and resisted by the professionals supporting her in their different roles. As I had found in the therapeutic observation with Rahan, here too the observer's role involved an extra effort to "get in" and to "stay connected", particularly as the time for the move away from the foster home approached.

In the aftermath of the deaths of her parents, describing developments in Ania from the observations in the foster home provided a focus for communication and reconnection at times when the network had fragmented. It was as if a kernel of living growth provided a nucleus around which more hopeful and living relationships could reform. The undivided attention given to Ania seemed to awaken a profound response in her that helped to create hope for both Sharon and Martina. This suggested that over the two years of the therapeutic observation, Ania had been able to take in experiences of being fully attended to that may help to sustain her in the move to a new family in another country and the challenges ahead of her.

## Danny

Danny, who was four years old, had been in foster care for eighteen months during care proceedings to decide on his future care. After a placement order for adoption was granted, the search for adoptive parents began. During this time, a younger foster sibling had moved away from the foster home to be adopted. Danny's social worker worried about the impact on him of neglectful and chaotic parenting in his family home before he was removed into care and of the separation from his parents and siblings, followed by the loss of the younger child who had left the foster family. Moments when Danny became very withdrawn and hard to reach had led to concerns about possible autistic spectrum difficulties. The social worker also worried that his foster carer, Farisa, may perhaps have had her hands and her mind "too full", with several young children coming and going from her care in previous years. She hoped for support to help Farisa to respond to Danny's deeper emotional needs during the long wait for an adoptive family. Another aim was for the therapeutic observations to help to inform the choice of and support for adoptive parents who would be able to allow Danny to attach to them at a pace that he could manage and who would be able to make use of psychological support.

Tall and thin, with a shock of red hair, Danny was a child who moved stiffly and who seemed young and old at the same time. Farisa found him a rewarding child to look after. He could be lively and affectionate and he thrived in the company of her young grandchildren. But she also commented that at times he acted as if he could not see or hear her, seeming to have completely shut down and leaving her feeling worried and at a loss. At nursery, staff reported that he tended to stay on his own, could not join in with the other children's play, and often seemed lost in the large group.

My colleague, clinical psychologist and infant mental health practitioner Marta Bacigalupi, visited him at the foster home and at his nursery over a period of four months.

*First impressions:* "Now, I'm doing my own play"

> Farisa welcomes me very warmly, she's very kind and maternal with Danny, who calls her "mum". . . . Danny looks older than his age, he's tall, thin, with red hair standing out from his face. He seems to be strong and full of energy, although his face looks pale and he's got dark shadows under his eyes.

The house was warm, orderly, and full of light. Danny's room was cosy and felt lived-in.

> He asks me to play with him. I join in with enthusiasm, but after a game that lasts a few seconds he seems bored and goes to take another toy. . . . He suggests making a necklace and asks Farisa to get the box with the beads. She asks, "Are you making a necklace for me?" Danny does not answer but opens the box with the coloured beads, throws them on the floor, and then turns his back to us, saying with a metallic voice, "Now I'm doing my own play."

Marta was struck by Danny's "metallic", mechanical-sounding voice. She noticed too that when he invited Farisa or her to join him in play and then turned his back, how she and Farisa were left feeling shut out and filled up with task of gathering up the beads that had been scattered all over the floor.

In Marta's first observation at the nursery, she was concerned by the lack of any visible pleasure and by something that seemed compulsive in Danny's play.

> Danny goes around with a plastic hammer, pretending to fix something in the wall and whispering, "I'm fixing the wall." . . . He wanders around, never looking directly at anyone, and holding several toys in his hands. When he finds a long piece of sticky tape, he holds it in front of his eyes, as if it was an invisible barrier between him and the outside world. The nursery worker tells me that when he is angry or sad he sits tearfully in a corner.

It seemed that Danny could only manage to remain in the busy room by staying close to the walls and holding on to objects that were hard or sticky. There was something very bleak in the way he seemed so alone in the middle of the lively group of children. Marta felt a strong wish to help him to play with the other children, but he seemed almost blind to their existence. Marta discussed her observations and heard about small changes the workers had noticed over the time he had been in the nursery. Like Farisa, the nursery staff found that it sometimes took an effort to bring Danny to mind, as if there was something not fully present in his way of being with others. Perhaps in his first months and years he had rarely had the experience of making an impact on someone in a way that felt predictable and safe. Thinking about Danny's early history of neglect, when his basic needs must often have been overlooked amid the competing demands of older and younger siblings, helped to make sense of this shadowy quality. The nursery staff came up with ways of supporting him by providing structured activities with other children in a small group for part of the day.

Marta reviewed the support for Danny in the nursery in telephone discussions while the observations continued in the foster home. Faced with being repeatedly left with feelings of emptiness that perhaps conveyed something of Danny's experiences of being overlooked and left behind, Marta tried to help Danny by linking together some of his present experiences. The start of this process was simply connecting one visit with the next.

> Danny asks me to play football with him: I am to be the goalkeeper. I position myself in front of the bed saying that it is the goal. He kicks the ball two or three times and I kick it back to him, showing genuine fun. But he gives up, sits down, turning his back, and silently starts to play with some building blocks. I feel dropped, and I have to make an effort to go on watching his play.

By remaining interested and friendly, Marta tried to show Danny that painful feelings of frustration and rejection can be survived. Some changes were already apparent in the third observation: Danny's play was becoming more imaginative and more sustained. With Farisa's help he was beginning to make more links between the past and the present.

> Danny and Farisa are both at the kitchen table. Danny greets me. There is a big pizza in the middle, with tomato and olives. I comment happily that

they have made it as they promised last time. Danny is very proud of himself and tells me how he made it. Farisa underlines that he likes it soft and helps him by reminding him what the ingredients are. It's a lovely moment of coming together, and I feel encouraged that the idea we talked about last time was kept in mind for two weeks.

As well as taking in and reflecting on her own experiences of being with Danny, Marta also tried to facilitate joint play between Danny and Farisa. She offered Farisa a space for thinking about him, while to Danny she offered the experience of another interested adult, responsive to his communications, both spoken and in his play. As the relationship between Danny and his foster carer deepened, Marta could gradually step back. Danny seemed more able to think and to express his wishes, and less afraid of relating with others.

It's a sunny day and we are playing in the garden, taking turns to be the doctor and the patient. Danny starts to put his biscuit crumbs in Farisa's cup of tea; she jokingly protests. He laughs and looks at his reflection in her cup.

It was as if Danny was giving little pieces of himself, the crumbs, to Farisa, for them to be reassembled and contained in her mindful, warm response to him. The gentle, tender quality of this play suggested that Danny had begun to take inside himself a reparative experience of being held in mind. In the last observations, Farisa shared with Marta her reflections on Danny's emotional states and her awareness and enjoyment of Danny's development.

Farisa tells me that last week Danny found a picture of her when she was pregnant with her daughter. He asked her if he came from her tummy too. She had taken the opportunity to show him his family photograph album. Immediately Danny runs inside to get the album. We look at the pictures carefully, and I'm pleased to see that Danny is able to look back to his past when he feels held by Farisa and me, without cutting off from his feelings as I had seen so often before. . . .

Farisa tells me about the last few days; she was surprised that Danny was really excited during the Queen's Jubilee. She's happy to point out to me that for the first time he was able to talk about something that happened to him in the nursery: he told her about a friend of his who had met the Queen.

In Marta's last visit to the nursery, the staff reported gradual but clear signs of improvement: Danny was now able to play with other children in a small group with adult support, and his attention span had increased. His play had become more meaningful and more sustained. He seemed more "present" and less prone to cut himself off. In the last observation visit, Danny was able to "play through" Marta's leaving.

> He starts to blow on my face, saying: "I am blowing you away" in a mixture of anger and playfulness. Then the anger grows and he tells me: "I'm locking you in a cage"; and then "a monster comes . . .". I knock on the table pretending to ask for help from inside the cage. Farisa asks him if he's going to rescue me, but instead he sits next to me, saying that now we're both locked in the cage. Then he, too, knocks on the table seeking for help.
>
> Farisa pretends she is coming with a bunch of keys to let us out. He says that it doesn't work and we are still locked in. At the third attempt, Danny says that Farisa's "golden key" has opened the cage. I feel flooded with relief and hopefulness.

In the last professional meeting with the social workers, we fed back on the work with Farisa and Danny and the nursery, and reflected on the future plans for Danny. We thought together about difficulties that might come up when the time came for him to move to a permanent placement, and how to support both Danny and Farisa's well-being during that time. Danny's social worker told us that the joint work and reflection had given her a deeper understanding of Danny's emotional needs and greater confidence about addressing the worries that had led her to refer him to the service.

Four months after the observation ended, adoptive parents came forward for Danny. They were able to welcome me as Marta's colleague to see Danny in his new home, and to bring together his new life with what was known about his early experiences. He was attending a small local primary school where his needs had been recognized and a programme of support was in place. I was moved to see photographs of Danny with Farisa and her family in his new home. It was heartening that these relationships were remembered and valued and to see him starting to settle in his new family.

### Discussion

Connecting the different external environments and people involved in his care, while at the same time holding in mind Danny's internal world, allowed Marta to create a therapeutic setting for the work in the foster home. Patterns of interaction that kept him isolated, and left those around him to take in experiences of feeling shut out or over-looked, could be recognized and made sense of. As Danny's play began to reflect the experience of being thought about and held in mind, it became lighter in feeling; there was a new sense of delight and wonder. The relief of finding mutual enjoyment may have helped both Danny and Farisa to live through the painful experience of separation that came with his adoption. This was an integrated experience of adoption; his adoptive parents were able to hold Danny's experiences and relationships in mind (Cregeen, 2017).

## A core dilemma: the complexity of belonging

Experiential knowledge gained through therapeutic observation allows us to understand more about the emotional complexity of fostering relationships and the spoken and unspoken dilemmas facing foster carers. We encounter the enormity of the impact of the child's arrival in the foster family and of the impact of loss when it is anticipated, when it happens, and after the child has gone.

Nadira seemed to "practise in her mind" at letting Rahan go, and, as the time finally came for him to be taken away, I had the sense that distress was regulated by means of a form of retreat that allowed her and her foster child moments of close contact alternating with with-drawal. For Sharon and for Farisa, there was greater confidence that some continuing relationship with their foster child might be possible. The links made between Sharon and Ania's grandparents allowed her to live through the experience of giving up her foster child with the reassurance of knowing whom she was going to be with and the significance of her relationship with Ania being acknowledged. For Farisa and Danny, there seemed to be a recognition, at once poignant and playful, of his having been taken in by her as he gazed at his reflection in her cup of tea.

# CHAPTER SIX

# Briefer interventions: Watch Me Play!

Watch Me Play! is an opportunity for the voice of the child to be heard through their play.

[Feedback from a child's social worker]

I n this chapter, I describe a briefer way of working that brings together the close attention of therapeutic observation with a more directive focus on child-led play. Sam, the five-year-old son of friends, provided a name for this intervention. When he asked me one Saturday morning to "Shut the door and watch me play!", he perfectly summarized his expectation of attention to his play in a contained space.

When a child comes into care, the circumstances are always complex. The importance of play for children's development can easily become lost in this crisis. The necessary focus on medical treatment and the need to ensure the safety of a child who has been injured can also, inadvertently, divert attention from the child's psychological and emotional needs. It may also be difficult for foster carers to go on reaching out to a child and making a meaningful emotional connection when a move away from the foster home is planned. At the same time, play that is led by the child can be particularly significant and helpful when there has been exposure to neglect and abuse or disrupted primary caregiving relationships. In the conflicted situations of children in care, play can provide a realm in which foster carer and child can come together at a pace that both can manage. For prospective adopters who may be looking for ways to connect with their child without overwhelming them, the boundaried realm of play may offer a space for sensitively exploring new relationships.

The Watch Me Play! approach involves creating an environment for exploratory play and learning from play that is led by the child. Creating an environment for play involves opportunities for the child to experience the undivided attention of their caregiver in a quiet space, with a selection of toys and materials that enable self-expression and creativity. Learning from the child's play means that the adult allows the child to take the lead, as long as what he or she chooses to do is safe. This way of working also brings together the adults who are involved with the child to reflect on what they see in the child's play and on how it feels to be with the child while he or she is playing. The case studies in this chapter illustrate the development of this approach. Practice considerations and learning about trainings, drawing on feedback from participants in Watch Me Play! workshops and focus groups are set out in chapter 7.

## Children who "cannot play"

Some children, when they first enter care, are described as unable to play. Kyle was three and half and his sister Bella a year younger when they were taken into care from hospital. They had experienced physical assaults that resulted in fractures. They had also witnessed violence between their parents, and both were very underweight. It was clear from their behaviour and their responses to adults that their basic needs had been severely neglected. They shied away from adults, clinging to each other for safety, and they were frightened of water. Both children also suffered from night terrors and feeding difficulties.

Kyle and Bella were placed in an emergency placement with Susanne, a foster carer who usually looked after teenagers, until carers could be found who had more experience with young children. By the time potential longer term foster carers had been identified, both children had formed such a close bond with Susanne that it was decided they should stay with her until their permanent placement was decided by the court. A support plan was agreed in a consultation with the children's social worker, who was particularly concerned about their disturbed feeding pattern and about whether Susanne would be able to continue to look after them. Direct work in the foster home would inform thinking with the social worker about the children's needs and, in due course, about how best to support a transition, whether a return to their parents' care or a move to an adoptive family.

When I phoned Susanne to introduce myself and offer a visit to the foster home, I heard about her first impressions: she described the children's arrival as "like a tornado hitting us". In my first visit, I saw and felt what she meant as the two children hurtled around the room making ear-piercing shrieks. There was much that felt confusing. Despite the difference in their ages, the two children were very similar in appearance: both slender and wiry, their faces half covered by curly brown hair. Although I was a complete stranger, they met me with huge smiles, while their wide, dark eyes seemed unfocused; they seemed to gaze in my direction rather than look at me. The impact of the trauma that these children had experienced felt overwhelming, and it was hard to know where to begin.

Susanne had the support of her adult daughter, Miriam, and the children's social worker and health visitor were committed to helping the placement to succeed. I spent time in the foster home taking in what it was like to be with the children. Kyle and Bella quickly adapted to the consistent routines of the foster home. At first terrified of being washed, with Susanne's patient reassurance they began to enjoy bath times. This seemed encouraging, but their high-pitched shrieks and relentless flitting from one toy to another were exhausting for Susanne and Miriam. It was difficult to believe that either child could ever drop their guard enough to make new relationships or to explore their world in play.

There were many battery-operated toys in the foster home, but I encouraged Susanne and Miriam to put these to one side and, instead, to provide a small number of soft toys and some cushions and to talk to the children quietly about what they did with the toys, and sometimes to sing to them. I was very moved in my next visit to see Bella for the first time lying still in Miriam's lap, listening raptly to a nursery rhyme.

In my fourth visit to the foster home, while I sat on the floor watching the children, Susanne commented that first Kyle and then Bella paused fleetingly to glance at me, before taking off again. I wondered if the children were showing an interest because I was giving them my full attention, and because, while I was sitting on the floor, they could see I would not suddenly move away. This seemed a good moment to explore the possibility of providing short periods of time each day when Susanne and Miriam could sit with Kyle or Bella and watch each

child and talk to him or her about their play. Susanne was frankly
sceptical about how this could help, but at the same time she was
ready to try anything. She and Miriam made time in their busy routines to provide Kyle and Bella with their undivided attention for five
or ten minutes once or twice a day. We worked together to create a
quiet and comfortable environment with a small number of simple toys
and a few cushions, putting away the battery-operated toys and turning the television off.

Kyle and Bella had been living on high alert, and it took many
months for the first signs of trusting relationships with their new
carers to be seen. I suggested that Susanne and Miriam allow each
child to take the lead in their play, decide what they were doing, even
if the play was very repetitive, as long as what they were doing was
safe, and to describe in a quiet commentary what they could see happening in the play. My visits alternated with prearranged phone calls
when I could ask Susanne about themes and developments in the children's play, and about what it was like to be with them while they
were playing. Had anything changed—or did things stay the same?
Was it lively—or did it make the adult with the child feel anxious,
bored, or upset? Susanne described how Kyle repeatedly crashed cars
together; this was followed by a period when the cars were pushed
under a sofa and he would ask Susanne to find them for him. Susanne
described the deadening, controlling atmosphere of this very repetitive
play: ten minutes was as much as she could manage. He rarely played
with other toys. When Susanne tried to distract him by showing him a
family of wooden dolls, he smashed one on top of the other with a
suddenness and force that felt shocking. Susanne's instinctive response
was to tell him to be nice and play with the dolls gently. Later, we
were able to think together about this sudden glimpse of something
that felt shocking and had the almost-real quality of a flashback.

Drawing on what was known of Kyle's early history, we reflected on
how his play might express something about terrifying experiences of
unpredictable adults and the drastic changes in his young life. I asked
Susanne if she could allow him to continue with his play without changing the direction of it, as long as what he was doing was safe, even
when it felt uncomfortable or disturbing to see. Susanne told me that it
had helped to be able to talk about what it was like to be with Kyle at
these times and how she was left feeling. As Kyle's early experiences
were communicated through his play and then thought about by
Susanne and myself, something changed. His experiences of being
frightened and of being rigidly controlled had been taken in. Susanne

was rewarded by seeing marked improvements in Kyle's pleasure in food and a more varied diet. There was less of the running around and high-pitched shrieking that had felt so exhausting. There were rewards as well for Kyle: he seemed less wary and began to seek comfort from her. For longer moments, he was able to relax when Susanne cradled him in her lap, rather than holding himself stiffly or pushing her away.

The moment when Susanne told me that Kyle had started to find his cars for himself marked an important development. The feeling of being with him had changed and had become more hopeful. They both enjoyed his newly found sense of his own agency and his new confidence. With Susanne sitting on the floor alongside him, Kyle now began to explore other toys. He avoided the doll family, but he now talked in a lively voice to the toy animals, and he joined in with singing nursery rhymes.

Care proceedings lasted over a year while assessments were carried out of Kyle and Bella's parents and members of their extended family. These proved to be negative, and the proceedings concluded with orders for the children to be adopted. During this time, first Kyle and later Bella were gradually introduced to nursery. Kyle developed a particular attachment to one of the nursery staff. Bella began to show a particular love of singing in her small group at nursery. When adoptive parents came forward for the two children, I was able to contribute from my observations and the work with Susanne and Miriam to planning an integrated transition to the adoptive family.

Having observed the depth of the attachment between the children and Susanne and the gradual introduction that had been needed before they felt safe in the new environment of the nursery, I was able to advocate for a slower than usual transition to the adoptive home and for continuing visits from Susanne to the children in the first months after their move. The children's adoptive parents were keen to hear about what had helped for Kyle and Bella and were interested to try the play support that the children had got used to in the foster home. This provided another thread of continuity and helped the children and their new parents to get to know each other.

In the course of intermittent telephone support for another two years with the adoptive parents, I had the pleasure of hearing about two children who were thriving in a stable and loving family environment. Kyle became fascinated by how plants grow. I heard that he loved to dig alongside his father in their allotment and had started planting his own vegetables. Bella still loved singing and music of all kinds; she had the confidence to sing in front of her class at school.

*Thinking together about play*

For carers looking after children who have had profoundly frightening experiences, reflecting together with someone who also sees the child and what happens in his or her play can provide companionship. This can help carers to remain open to sometimes disturbing states of mind that the children let them know about in their behaviour and through their play. The play of traumatized children can have a mind-numbing quality: toy cars being repeatedly crashed together; toys being thrown, suddenly, or over and over again; or a game being broken off by the child as soon as the adult joins in. Something that feels joyless, driven, and relentless in a child's play can be hard to stay with. Carers may feel paralysed by the experience of something being re-enacted, over and over again, leaving child and carer feeling ever more isolated from each other.

The focus on play seemed to help Susanne and Miriam to reach past the wariness of children who had learned to avoid adult attention. Setting aside the time to take in and reflect on something that felt highly controlled in the children's play allowed something to shift and brought something new into their relationship with their carers. The children's feelings and ideas and their ways of expressing them were now seen as important. Expressing themselves through their play while being confident of being held in mind by their foster carers provided outlets for long-held-in tensions. Continuing this approach with their adoptive parents provided another strand of continuity for the children and helped the adoptive parents to feel that they were able to attune to the children at a pace that they could manage.

Social workers and legal professionals have reported that direct observations of children help to bring the children's emotional experiences and psychological needs to life during care proceedings. This can be all the more important when the adults in the family themselves have long-unmet needs that could become the main focus of attention. Thinking together about observations of the children's play and the small but significant changes that can be seen over time allows care-planning discussions to be informed by and focused on the children's needs.

## "The house feels lighter"

Noemi, two and a half years old, and her foster carer, Jade, both appeared depressed when I met them following concerns that the care being provided in the foster home was "functional" and lacking in warmth. Noemi and her sister Anita, three years older, came into care when their mother Tina was taken into hospital after collapsing in the street. Following the acrimonious break up of her relationship with the children's father, Tina had suffered from severe depression since Noemi's birth and had become reliant on alcohol. Child protection social workers had been concerned that at times, five-year-old Anita took on the weight of responsibility for looking after her mother and her baby sister.

Jade was shocked by how hungry the children were when they arrived in her home. She was also appalled by the amount of physical fighting and the relentlessness of the rivalry between the sisters. They must have often been hungry, frightened, or in discomfort, with no hope of someone to turn to. As a result of her alcohol dependence and her severe depression, their mother was likely to have responded to them unpredictably and at times in ways that were frightening. Jade described having felt isolated with the struggle of trying to establish routines for the children and to begin to get to know them in the first weeks of the foster placement. She had been taken aback when Noemi "iced her out" or scratched or bit her in sudden moments of rage or aggression that seemed to come out of the blue.

When I met Noemi and Jade for a session in the clinic playroom, I was struck by Noemi's stiff gait and the way she held herself apart from Jade. Noemi's hair was tightly plaited in neat cornrows with two bright pink ribbons that seemed to not quite fit with her sombre, slightly frowning expression. Coming into the clinic playroom, she glanced at the doll's house without moving towards it or looking or turning to Jade. The atmosphere in the room was heavy as I introduced myself and talked about having some time for Noemi to play, and for me and Jade to think about her. Later, I realized that Noemi had been completely silent for the first twenty minutes of the session.

I sat on the floor of the playroom and placed some toy animals and fences, wooden dolls, and a teddy bear near to Noemi. Slowly she picked up one animal after another and looked at it. In a loud voice, Jade began to tell Noemi the names of the animals and asked her to repeat them. Noemi turned away and stared into space. Jade told me that this was Noemi acting like a sulky teenager. I encouraged Jade to sit on the floor and suggested we just watch what Noemi chose to do and make a time to talk afterwards about what we had seen. When Jade sat down near her, Noemi took some cushions and a blanket and played at going to bed. Jade now talked to her in a quieter voice, describing what she was doing. In the next two sessions, Noemi repeated this game with increasing delight, and then she began to play peekaboo with Jade, hiding behind the blanket.

Later in the third session, Noemi lifted her arms to be picked up by Jade. I felt a deep relief as I saw her relax into Jade's lap, her rigid muscle tone softened. Noemi's sombre expression lifted more often now into a smile, and she vocalized more freely. Jade told me: "The house feels lighter." I heard that, in the foster home, Noemi had begun to play with a baby doll, sometimes insisting that Jade hold it while Noemi watched. It seemed important for Noemi to be able to see Jade's predictable, safe response over and over again. Thinking about Noemi's experiences allowed Jade to make links with Noemi's current behaviour and to see her more as a child, even younger in her emotional development than her actual age.

It felt very encouraging that Jade was able to join in with observing and taking an interest in Noemi's play. Noemi often seemed more able to accept comfort and nurture in indirect ways—for example, represented by the baby doll. Later, there began to be times when Noemi regressed, crawling and vocalizing like a baby. I thought that Noemi might have had powerful experiences of infantile needs that were unmet in her first months of life and were now being understood and responded to. I encouraged Jade to see these moments of regression as opportunities to catch up on missed early experiences and as indicating that Noemi was starting to feel safer. Noemi's social worker was able to support the helpfulness of responding to Noemi as to a much younger child at these times. We also thought about the very different times when Noemi behaved more like a much older child. Jade began to recognize a consistent pattern in which Noemi appeared most self-sufficient and dismissive of comfort in situations that repeated the stresses that she was likely to have experienced in earliest childhood. We saw many instances of Noemi rejecting help from Jade, while at the same time her need for affection and physical closeness was clear. Noemi may have found direct attention threatening because in the past she may have received unpredictable or frightening responses from her mother.

Jade reported that the sudden eruptions of aggression became less frequent. She became more able to anticipate situations that might create anxiety for Noemi, leading her to lash out or scratch. These often involved a small change in routine, something unexpected that Noemi could not anticipate, or even a change in the tone of Jade's voice. Thinking about Noemi's early history provided a background context for understanding how quickly something could begin to feel too much or not safe for Noemi. I was heartened to see that Noemi began to seek and accept more closeness with Jade, sometimes sitting in her lap and sometimes playing out a bedtime routine with increasingly lively smiles and a real sense of enjoyment. I thought these were positive signs of a developing trust and intimacy between Noemi and Jade.

## The continuing impact of early trauma and deprivation

> The very early and even pre-birth experiences of children in care often have a particularly damaging quality that is more significant and more enduring than any ordinary impingement. The patterns created by traumatic affective experiences in the pre-verbal stage of development, or primal repetitions, are exceptionally difficult to put into words, as they will most likely have their roots in experiences that were not only pre-verbal, but also "pre-imagistic". [Tiltina, 2015, p. 54]

Noemi's outbursts of sudden aggression seemed to come out of the blue, taking her carer by surprise and leaving her feeling at a loss. The unpredictability of her sudden changes of mood seemed to be linked to dysregulated states of mind that change suddenly and abruptly from one extreme to another. But there may also be something that feels profoundly "unthinkable" in the communications of young children who have not been helped to make sense of their first experiences of life and to put them into words. In ordinary development, the "dance" of attuned interaction between caregiver and baby soon leads to parents talking to their babies.

Putting feelings and thoughts into words is a very important way in which parents introduce the world to their baby a little at a time. Even though the baby doesn't understand the words, talking to the baby and describing the world around them can help the baby to get to know familiar sequences of activity and to link words to actions; talking about feelings allows the baby to experience the parent making painful feelings manageable in their own mind (Daws & de Rementeria, 2015). What was known of Noemi's early history suggested that she may have had few experiences of her emotional states being responded to and of hearing adults talking to her sensitively. Her older sister had, it seemed, tried to fill the gap for her and had provided some of her physical care, but there must have been many times when Noemi's discomfort and distress were too much for a six-year-old child to cope with.

Many factors can lead to foster carers becoming distant from the children they are looking after. Burn-out is a professional risk, under the impact of repeated, often unprocessed losses. Repeated experiences of rejection by children whose interactive styles appear indifferent or dismissive bring the risks of discouragement and of secondary trauma. Foster carers may feel unvalued in a climate that militates against validating the parenting that they provide. I did not have the scope to follow up this intervention, but it seemed that the transitional space of play and the experience of mutual delight that it afforded had allowed something to become freed up and created more warmth between carer and child.

## Finding a home

Three year-old Miguel came into care when it was recognized that attempts to support his teenage parents, Teresa and Leon, had not been successful enough to protect Miguel from frightening experiences and a lack of consistent care. His young parents struggled with learning difficulties, which meant that they also struggled to understand the needs of their baby son. Providing consistent care for him was difficult for them, and he often went hungry. The young parents moved frequently with their baby between different providers of supported housing, never remaining in one place for more than a few months. On several occasions, Miguel witnessed his young mother being shouted at and hit by men who exploited her vulnerability.

Miguel's parents' response to the support they were offered by social workers varied. At times they welcomed, or indeed demanded, help to manage the practicalities of looking after themselves and their son but they also found the involvement of social services hard to tolerate. When they made complaints about workers assigned to support the family, the worker was changed in an effort to sustain an ongoing partnership. The young parents' own unmet needs were so prominent that it may have been hard at times for a new worker, anxious about maintaining a relationship with parents who were very sensitive to feeling intruded on, to hold Miguel in mind too. As a result, Miguel had four different social workers before he was taken into foster care. I understood that he was a compliant child who did not draw attention to himself by temper tantrums or displays of defiance.

Miguel was first placed in care, with his parents' agreement, following a crisis when they found themselves homeless once again. He was looked after by an emergency foster carer for two weeks until a longer term foster carer was found. He seemed to settle well with the latter foster family, but after three months the foster carer had to leave the country when her father fell seriously ill. Now aged three and a half, Miguel was moved to a third foster placement. Sadly his new foster carer was herself profoundly depressed and felt burnt out. She felt that she had not recovered from the loss of a baby girl whom she had fostered from birth until she was taken away very suddenly two years earlier.

In this foster placement, adequate physical care was provided, but the foster carer was unable to provide Miguel with affection or stimulation. He was well-fed and dressed in clean clothes, but was left alone for much of the day in front of the television with a few broken toys. His social worker faced a difficult dilemma: she was reluctant to put him through yet another change of placement, but she could see that he was experiencing a repetition of the emotional neglect that he had suffered as a baby.

My involvement began with a consultation with the social worker in which we put together a timeline of the main events and changes in Miguel's life and planned a series of observations and visits. When I visited Miguel in the foster home, I met a sturdy child with a flat expression. He was lethargically kicking around a half-deflated football in the lounge and glancing from time to time at a large television screen. It was hard to believe he was only three years old. There was little interaction between him and his carer, but when she gave him a bowl of soup, which she had made with spices from her home country, he ate it avidly and told me he loved it. He struck me as a child who had a very strong capacity to take in whatever was good in his environment. He accepted my presence, and in my second and third visits began to play with toys that I brought, talking to himself in a low monotone that gave me the sad feeling that he was very used to being alone.

The staff at his nursery were worried about Miguel from his first day there, after he was left by the foster carer with no introduction. They contacted social services after his keyworker heard him calling himself a "bad boy" and hitting himself on the head. In his isolation and loneliness, it seemed that Miguel blamed himself for the losses in his life and perhaps, too, for his mother's depression. Although there were concerns straight away about his well-being, it seemed difficult to think about Miguel and to hold him in mind. All kinds of delays got in the way of the usual meetings that take place between professionals when a child in care starts at nursery. It was as if the learning difficulties that occluded his mother's parenting had somehow become replicated in a network around him that was unable to think about him or to communicate.

The observations helped to inform the care planning for Miguel and were also helpful a few weeks later when his social worker left and there was another change of social worker. After some weeks, when it became apparent that very little change had been seen in the quality of his care, the decision was taken for him to be moved to a couple who could give Miguel the nurturing attention and affection he needed. I visited him in the second week of his new foster placement with Alejandro and Luciana. The atmosphere in the foster home was warm and welcoming. Alejandro and Luciana shared the worry with me early on that Miguel was "too good". They worried that it might be hard for them to get to know what he needed and wanted because he seemed so careful around them. But even in my first visits, Miguel seemed to me to have become more like a child. His facial expression had lost some of its tense wariness; he intently watched Alejandro as he prepared the family meals. I heard that Miguel had not been seen hitting himself since he moved. Both Alejandro and Luciana joined Miguel in playing with toy cars on the floor. They wondered to me, when noticing how long and complicated these car games became, if something was being replayed here of Miguel's journey to a loving foster home.

Protracted care proceedings had concluded with a placement order for Miguel to be adopted, but he was now nearly six and no adoptive family had come forward for him. He had been living with Alejandro and Luciana for eight months when his care plan was changed from adoption to long-term foster care. Miguel was a rewarding child to look after who was much loved in his foster family. He had been able to hold on in his mind to an idea of someone who could be a parent to him throughout the many disruptions in his young life. He had remained emotionally available and able to be helped by his foster carers, despite the early disruptions in his care and his repeated placement moves. His capacities to take in the good and to communicate eloquently about his emotional experiences were rich internal resources that seemed to have helped him to keep going during periods of profound deprivation.

It was possible that my visits to him in his different placements, holding him in mind and giving him my full attention, had also helped in his psychological survival. The focus on play that seemed to help Miguel and his new foster carers to get to know each other also provided a way of linking with the many different professionals that it was necessary to liaise with, because of the repeated placement moves and changes in personnel. The intervention lasted almost a year. Alejandro and Luciana were able to form friendly and supportive relationships with Miguel's parents, Teresa and Leon, and joined them for some of their meals and contact outings together with Miguel. A consistent social worker who visited regularly could provide a child with the same all-important continuity.

Long-term work that moves through different phases and involves linking with successive foster carers and social workers also helps to inform briefer interventions that are also part of the remit of mental health services for children in care. The following brief intervention brought home to me how hard it must have been for a first-time foster carer to feel that she could be important for and close to the traumatized infant in her care.

## A child returning to the care of his family

The Watch Me Play! approach can underpin both brief and longer term interventions. In some instances, we have been able to follow a child from one temporary foster placement to another and, finally, to the permanent home with adoptive parents or special guardians, or with birth parents or kinship carer.

Samuel came into care when a special guardianship arrangement with his maternal great-aunt broke down after three years. It was difficult to find out about how he had come to live with her or why the placement had ended. We understood that his teenage mother had returned to Ghana and his father had broken off any contact with the family. Samuel was a shy four-year-old who spoke in a whisper and was quick to say please, sorry, thank you. He avoided any physical comfort from his thoughtful foster carer, Lee. A shift was seen after two Watch Me Play! sessions and telephone support in between. My colleague noticed that as soon as Samuel started to play, Lee made many suggestions about what he could do next. It seemed that Lee very much wanted to find a way of giving something to Samuel and, in doing so, at times unwittingly became intrusive. When Lee was able to take a step back and started to see how Samuel was then able to play more freely, a new side of Samuel began to emerge. Now he could show the toy animals fighting, shout when he was winning at Snap, and ask to be held on Lee's lap when he got upset. Lee felt that Samuel had come alive and had become a four-year-old child instead of a "mini-adult". He began to enjoy looking after Samuel much more, even when the placement became more challenging as Samuel became less compliant.

Care proceedings resumed when Samuel's paternal uncle Tony and his family came forward for him. They were assessed, and Samuel was placed with them after a period of introductions during which the foster family and Tony's family met up and got to know each other over a period of two months. A supervision order remained in place for a year. We were able to offer three more Watch Me Play! sessions. Lee had shared some of his experiences with Tony before Samuel moved to the family. Where Lee had at first honed in on Samuel's play with lots of suggestions, Tony's response in his first Watch Me Play! session was a bit different: he asked lots of questions about who was in the play, where they were going, why things happened. I was able to notice with Tony that each time a question was asked, Samuel stopped what he was doing, looked carefully at Tony, and silently moved on to doing something else. I suggested to Tony that he might see more of what was going on for Samuel if he simply repeated the few words that Samuel spoke and added a few words of his own, describing what he could see in Samuel's play. Avoiding questions beginning with "Wh . . .?" (who, what, where, why) seemed to help Samuel to express something in his play that he could not have put into words. He then moved to the toy telephone and repeatedly played a game where he made a pretend phone call to Tony but remained silent or slammed the phone down each time Tony responded with a friendly "Hello?". Tony, not unnaturally, found this play uncomfortable, but with encouragement he was able to allow it to continue so that we could see what would happen next. After a while, Samuel turned to the tea set and gave Tony several cups of pretend tea. Tony told me that he felt quite put out when Samuel "put the phone down on him" or responded with a silence, and his inclination had been to put a stop to the play. But when Samuel gave him the cups of tea he felt that he was being rewarded in some way and given something nice.

We wondered together both about Samuel's first experiences before going into the care of his great-aunt, a time about which little was known, and about his life with his great-aunt before his placement with her broke down. Samuel's cautious and extremely polite behaviour when he first came to live with Lee suggested that he may have learned early to be very careful around adults and that his own needs and wishes may have often had to wait. In this brief intervention, the focus on play and attention seemed to help Samuel and his foster carer and then his uncle to find each other. There was an extra strand of continuity for Samuel in that he had got used to doing Watch Me Play! every day for twenty minutes with Lee, and Tony had been able to continue the same routine at least for the first few months after Samuel came to his care.

## "Do I matter to her?"

The mother of Amy was twenty weeks pregnant when a pre-birth assessment found that the risks to her unborn baby met the threshold for a care order. In the last nine years, four previous children had been taken into care and subsequently adopted. The risks were cumulative, stemming from her mother's mental health difficulties and substance abuse and a series of abusive relationships with violent partners. During the pregnancy, Amy's mother had returned to a relationship with a previous partner, who had been violent to her in the past. Amy's father had a history of convictions for drugs offences, domestic violence, and attacks on police officers. He was in prison at the time that Amy was born.

Amy was exposed to heroin and alcohol in the womb. Domestic violence, repeated moves, and her father's conviction during the pregnancy were among stress factors for her mother while she was pregnant with Amy. Amy's mother also suffered from depression, and she had become socially isolated; her partner's controlling and at times intimidating behaviour had led to her family and friends becoming estranged.

Amy remained in hospital for three weeks while withdrawing from heroin, looked after by the nurses on the ward, until she was moved to her foster placement. No one in her extended family was able to come forward to be assessed as a kinship carer for her. The day after she arrived in the foster placement, the foster carer, Donna, had to take the three-week-old baby on a 90-minute journey to have supervised contact with her mother in the local authority contact centre. The contact, ordered by the family court for the purposes of maintaining a relationship with her mother, took place four times a week.

By entering care at birth, Amy was protected from the possibility of exposure to domestic violence or physical abuse, and she was provided with good physical care in a safe and clean environment. She was faced with only one change of primary caregiver, from her mother to her foster carer; but she was looked after by multiple caregivers while in hospital, and in her first few weeks she encountered more adults than a typically developing child would, including the contact supervisors, her social worker, the foster carer's supervising social worker, as well as the foster carer's immediate family. The contact with her mother meant that she was out of her home for five hours for four days a week. This made it difficult for the foster carer to settle with her into a stable routine. It also meant that Amy experienced different styles of caregiving, from her foster carer and from her mother.

Amy was five months old when concerns were expressed about her shrill, persistent crying and sudden mood changes. When I visited the foster placement, it was hard for me to hear over the sound of a large television nearby as Donna described her worries. I noticed that Amy was surrounded by battery-operated toys making random, piercing sounds and flashing lights as she pressed their buttons. I saw that Amy repeatedly glanced briefly in Donna's direction after a particularly loud noise, then dropped her gaze when Donna was looking elsewhere. As this went on, Amy's face became paler and her arms and legs seemed to stiffen. It seemed to me that Donna may have lost, or perhaps had never had, the confidence that her presence and attention were important for Amy.

This was a brief intervention in which I had the opportunity to think with Donna and the supervising social worker supporting her about what might help Amy to regulate her high levels of arousal and help Donna to tune into Amy's signals. I was also able to follow up with Donna and with Amy's social worker by telephone for the next six weeks.

I encouraged Donna to consider turning the television off for some of the time and putting away the mechanical toys. I wondered with Donna about how all the technological equipment in the hospital might have left her feeling that electronic toys were what Amy needed. The long journeys to the contact centre seemed to put a tremendous strain on Donna; perhaps in this way she was identifying with a baby whose early development was compromised by maternal stress.

Reflecting together, and validating the care that she could provide, seemed to help to create the conditions for a quieter environment, in which Donna could hold Amy in her arms, talk quietly or sing to her, and watch, and get to know her rapid, fleeting facial expressions (American Academy of Pediatrics, 2012). Encouraging Donna to provide Amy with her undivided attention for regular periods of ten or twenty minutes at a time increased Donna's belief that she could provide something important and nurturing for a foster baby who had seemed worryingly withdrawn. Donna became more confident about being able to see when Amy was ready for play and when she needed to rest. It also helped Amy to send clearer signals and cues to the caregiver whose attention was now on her.

Repeatedly receiving familiar responses in the transitional space provided by play brings the experience that Frances Tustin calls a "rhythm of safety" (1986; see also Winnicott, 1951). Donna reported to her social worker that she felt she was getting to know Amy in a different way. Pleasurable interactions began to be described as Amy began to seek Donna's attention, her long gazes giving way to slow smiles as Donna talked to her and waited for her response. Donna began to recognize stress factors for Amy, and she felt more able to anticipate her changes of mood and more confident about soothing her when she was upset.

## Watch Me Play! as part of an assessment

The Watch Me Play! approach grew out of the experience that sharing direct and detailed observations of children's play brings something alive in professional networks or care proceedings. When this approach is not successful, efforts may need to go into gathering a team around the child before direct work with child and carer can begin. Watch Me Play! can also help to identify when a wider professional intervention may be required—for example, when emotional receptivity or warmth is lacking in the care given to a child. Earlier in this chapter, I described Miguel's experience in a foster home, where he was provided with adequate physical care but lacked the responsive nurture that healthy development requires; a foster carer who was preoccupied with previous losses was unable to be emotionally available to him. After a period in which support was offered to the foster carer but little change was seen, a prepared move was planned for Miguel, to a foster carer who was able to be more proactive and sensitive to the needs of a young child with so many disadvantages.

Another complex situation that may call for wider multidisciplinary intervention comes about when child maltreatment is utterly denied despite the evidence of significant harm that has led to a child being removed from parents. Denial makes it difficult for a child to accept substitute care and removes the possibility of understanding. When children who have been maltreated have frequent contact with parents who deny harming them, work with the parents by social workers, together with legal advice, may be needed to protect children from continuing to be exposed to intractable conflicts that can have serious consequences for mental health. Foster placements and contact with birth families are most likely to bring positive outcomes for children when parents are able to accept the child's need to be in care and, painful as this may be, give their support to the foster carers (Neil & Howe, 2004). When this cannot happen, irreconcilable conflicts of loyalties can leave children painfully divided and unable to accept nurture and affection from their foster carers.

## Trauma, play, and recovery

Many children respond to consistent and reliable attention from an adult in ways that are lively, imaginative, and eloquent. But it takes time and effort to sift through the impact of unspoken communications that may convey aspects of children's early experiences. Skilled and sensitive support is needed to enable foster carers and social workers to go on reaching out to the children in their care despite receiving discouraging or contradictory responses and despite the accumulated stresses that can result in secondary trauma. The focus on attending to a child's play can help to bring together a team around the child and carer. A social worker whose relationship with a child brought her into contact with very upsetting feelings about the child's early experiences reflected that "working together gives me hope for the future". When adults are able to see the reality of a child's experiences, the child is less alone with his or her distress; the impact of the child's trauma is mitigated.

In the case studies I have described, the focus on play seemed at times to help to bring hope where hope was hard to find, and to allow professionals to take in the reality of the distress experienced by a young child without being overwhelmed. As McFadyen (1994) comments in relation to work in neonatal units, observational approaches provide opportunities to integrate thinking about children's developmental and psychological needs in a way that can feel tolerable rather than critical or persecutory. Thinking together as a cohesive group of professionals can then help to regulate the stress and pain of accepting the reality and severity of the traumas that lead to young children entering care. Seeing different ways in which the impact of trauma is shown can be combined with noticing more hopeful signs of progress in a child's development and relationships. Recognizing both the small encouraging steps forward and the difficulties that may still get in the way of recovery brings a more integrated understanding of the adversities facing a child and his or her strengths. In this way, reflection based on observation can help to bring about more integrated states of mind in networks that help professionals to be imaginative and hopeful while remaining grounded in reality.

# CHAPTER SEVEN

# Practice considerations for the Watch Me Play! approach

A s the case examples in chapter 6 indicate, Watch Me Play! is a flexible approach that can help children to feel that they are held in mind—a fundamental aspect of ordinary parenting that can be adversely impacted by the anxieties and uncertainties of life in care. Attention and play are complementary: observing with warmth and interest helps to facilitate the child's play. As the child's play becomes more focused and meaningful, it becomes easier for adults to remember and think about the child's communications. Providing an environment for child-led play allows us to learn from the child when to reach out to make emotional contact and when to stand back, remaining available and interested, until the child is ready to make a connection. Close observation of the child's communications in play in turn informs the reflection that allows professionals to provide containment and a child-focused perspective in care planning. As one social worker commented, "Watch Me Play! helps the social worker to see the world through the child's eyes."

Watch Me Play! promotes play that is led by the child together with undivided attention from his or her caregiver. The aim is to establish a routine of regular play sessions of around twenty minutes two or more times a week. The approach also involves two kinds of talking: talking with the child about what he or she does in his or her play allows feelings and ideas to be put into words; talking with another adult about the child's play allows caregivers to reflect together on their discoveries and on the delights and worries in the experience of being with the child. Children who have not been consistently held in mind in their earliest infancy may evoke feelings in others that are raw, unpredictable, or hard to think about. Sharing observations, making connections, celebrating developments, and puzzling over surprises with a fellow foster carer, family member, social worker, or clinician can help to regulate the impact of these feelings.

In a project funded by the Tavistock Clinic Foundation, I discussed the Watch Me Play! approach with professionals—including social workers, foster carers, contact supervisors, and mental health clinicians —and with adoptive parents across the UK (Wakelyn, 2018, 2019). The practice guidance in this chapter draws on discussions in these workshops and focus groups.

There was widespread agreement among participants that an early intervention for babies and young children in care is needed: "All the evidence suggests the earlier you intervene the better—rather than waiting for children to act up when they are 7, 8, 9—or 17." Advocacy for babies and young children who have experienced psycho-social difficulties was also recognized as part of the task of professionals in the care system: one participant poignantly commented: "They are this kind of forgotten." Another participant described a blanking out of the emotional lives of infants and young children that was widely recognized across professions and from different regions: "People put 'not applicable' as the answer to questions about the emotional state when it's a baby."

Professionals and adoptive parents alike welcomed the opportunity in Watch Me Play! for children to express themselves, make choices, and develop a sense of their own agency: "This is the one area where the child does have some control, in their play." The focus on play was identified as "valuable, but all too easily overlooked"; early years and health practitioners commented that the core topics of observation and play, although central in their trainings, needed to be rediscovered and revisited in the complex contexts of children in care. Another social worker fed back that: "The routines are attended to, but play is always a gap". Placing the focus on play that is led by the child, rather than by the caregiver giving directions and instructions, felt important: a foster carer commented, "Not intervening can lead to a story being told by a child through play." The significance of enhancing mutual enjoyment in the relationship between child and carer was also highlighted by a child's social worker:

This could allow foster carers to get more enjoyment from being with the children. It could help the carers to feel involved and the children to feel they are wanted. That could help the children to feel the carers aren't just doing it because it's their job.

## Creating an environment for play

Playfulness takes different forms at each stage of development. The youngest babies become fully alert in face-to-face interactions with a parent or carer, each watching the other closely (Daws & de Rementeria, 2015; Murray & Andrews, 2005). Later in infancy, touching games such as "Round and round the garden", "Pat-a-cake" or "One potato—two potato" that produce fun and laughter provide moments of safe, predictable physical contact for infants whose earliest experiences may have been frightening. Peekaboo, hide-and-seek, and other teasing games that often evolve naturally allow for exploration of the adult's reactions and of experiences of coming and going that are important for later turn-taking, self-regulation, and social relationships (Reddy & Mireault, 2015).

Exploratory play, making a mess, or getting things "wrong" are important ways in which children learn about their environment and develop the skills in coordination and communication that underpin later formal learning. Mind-mindedness research has demonstrated that thinking about meaning helps children to be able to communicate and to learn: children whose caregivers ascribe meaning to their first sounds and gestures go on to know more words at the age of five years (Meins & Fernyhough, 2010; Meins et al., 2003).

Establishing a play routine involves planning a time in advance and providing a quiet space for child-led play with the television off and phones and screens put away. It is also important to give the child some advance warning a few minutes before the end of the play session, as well as to work out a way to finish the session that leaves the child looking forward to the next time. Foster carers and adoptive parents have commented on the importance of creating a consistent routine that is manageable and realistic, so that children have regular opportunities to experience attention to their play. A shorter time a few times a week is more beneficial than a more ambitious routine that cannot be sustained.

For some children, the opportunity for free play may provide an outlet for long-held-in feelings, which may include aggression or overwhelming confusion. Carers are encouraged to accept the child's play and to talk over what they see with another adult—a family member, another carer, a health visitor, or a social worker. Play that is felt to be disturbing or upsetting to watch and does not change over time is an indication that seeking professional advice should be considered. Some caregivers may feel they have more of a teaching role even with young children, which can make it hard to let the child take the lead and freely explore. Trainings and support sessions can provide guidance from child development research on the value of imaginative play and exploration, providing the foundations for the skills for later learning.

## Introducing Watch Me Play! in practice

Watch Me Play! can be introduced in different ways. Guidance leaflets (see Boxes 7.1 and 7.2 and the manual (Wakelyn, 2019) for examples) can be discussed with foster carers in trainings, meetings, and health assessments. Foster carers can be supported by supervising social workers and peer-support networks as well as by children's social workers. Health visitors may be able to support parents and caregivers in the home.

## Toys and play materials

Many children who are described as unable to play, or whose play mainly consists of throwing or destroying toys, are more able to engage in sustained play when they are in a quiet space with the full attention of the caregiver, with toys that are appropriate for the child's developmental level. It may be harder for children who have been maltreated to find and follow their own thought processes and to focus on a single activity. They can be helped by being provided with simple toys that let them use their imagination, such as small wooden dolls, toy animals, a toy tea set, and a toy telephone. A screen-free environment for much of the day is essential for children who may have developmental difficulties. Battery-operated toys can also be overstimulating and particularly distracting for children whose early experiences have led them to be hypervigilant and who are unconsciously constantly scanning their environment for threat.

The list in Box 7.3 gives some suggestions. Play often takes the same form over and over and over again, sometimes with a slight variation, sometimes exactly the same. These repetitions help us to notice and pick up the signals of infants and young children who may have learned in their earliest relationships to keep quiet in order to evade adult attention. Responding to these signals with affection and consistency helps to

Box 7.1

---

**Why Play Matters**

Wanting to play is natural—for everyone: babies, growing children, and adults.

Having fun together is important. But play isn't just about fun. When a baby watches an adult's face or listens to their voice, he or she is starting to learn.

**When we play we learn to:**

> Explore
> Focus
> Concentrate
> Pay attention
> Imitate someone
> Try out something new
> Do the same thing hundreds of times
> Find out about our own feelings
> Get to know another person
> Learn what we can do
> Take turns
> Pretend
> Wait
> Imagine
> . . .

**Being in tune, relaxed, and playful together helps babies to grow up healthy and secure. It's good for parents and carers too: playing together means growing together!**

---

introduce children to a new experience of relating to adults in a safe way.

## How can Watch Me Play! help?

Although it has been developed to address the needs of young children in temporary foster placements, the Watch Me Play! approach can also be used in a range of contexts. It can be helpful as a first-line intervention for children who may have had adverse experiences or who have

Box 7.2

---

**7 Top Tips for Watch Me Play!**

- Watch your child play—you'll get new ideas from him or her

- Make a regular "special play time" with your child

- Put out simple toys that let your child use his or her imagination

- Provide a quiet space for play, without TV or computers

- Help your child move to a new activity by singing a song together

- Keep your child's drawings and paintings in a special place or a folder

- If playing together feels hard to do, talk with another adult in the family, or to your health visitor

---

needs that are difficult to understand. The approach can also help to indicate whether more intensive assessment or interventions are needed and to identify support and training needs for caregivers. A manual for Watch Me Play! that will allow the approach to be

Box 7.3

---

**A Watch Me Play! Toy Kit**

Simple toys that allow children to express themselves, communicate, and explore their imagination allow more creative play and scope for development and communication than battery-operated or electronic devices. The following is a list of useful toys:

> Boxes, containers, wooden spoons
> Baby dolls, teddy bears, soft toys
> Doll's house and furniture, wooden dolls
> Toy animals
> Toy train, plastic vehicles
> Small blanket or rug, pillows or cushions.
> Plasticine and Play-Doh
> Toy tea set
> Toy telephones
> Plenty of plain paper for drawing, A4 or A3
> Coloured sugar paper for cutting up or making into folders

---

evaluated in different contexts is available at the Tavistock/First Step website (Wakelyn, 2019).

Foster carers have reported improvements in the play skills, mood, and behaviour of their foster children, and they have also described themselves feeling more confident about understanding the feelings and behaviour of the child in their care. The approach has also been found helpful in a wider range of contexts. A young care-leaver in a mother–baby placement commented on her eighteen-month-old son's delighted anticipation of his play sessions with her, once he had got used to a daily Watch Me Play! routine. A mother whose two-year-old son was returned to her after a period in foster care described him as calmer after three weeks of regular child-led play sessions; his play became more sustained, and she saw him concentrating for longer periods of time. Watch Me Play! can also provide a helpful element of continuity for children during and following a move to an adoption or special guardianship.

## The role of a Watch Me Play! clinician

Infant mental health clinicians who are trained in observation can model the Watch Me Play! approach with caregivers in the home or in the clinic, encouraging them to provide an environment conducive to free play and to allow the child to direct his or her own play. The frequency of Watch Me Play! sessions and the number of sessions offered can be adapted to fit the circumstances of children and caregivers. Some parents and carers have described positive changes after two or three sessions, while for some children and caregivers, six or eight sessions may be needed before changes are evident. If it does not prove possible to establish a play routine that is satisfactory for child and caregiver, or there are difficulties that have not changed after six or eight sessions, more intensive assessment and intervention are likely to be needed.

The central task for a Watch Me Play! clinician is to facilitate the caregiver's observations by observing alongside the caregiver, showing interest in his or her observations, and feeding back sensitively to the child and caregiver during the play session and with the caregiver afterwards. Noticing moments when there is a particularly strong emotional response can help to identify particular aspects of the child's play that may be especially helpful to think about more. A prearranged time to reflect with the carer after the play session—face to face or on the phone—provides opportunities to revisit these moments and discuss them together. This reflection on observation of the child's play and on the experience of being with the child while they play can help to generate a culture in the professional network that validates feelings and thinking about meaning.

Regularly providing children with undivided attention is second nature to many caregivers, while for others it may at first seem unnecessary or even unnerving. Not being in charge of the direction of play and being open to the child's imagination and ideas may be a very new stance for some caregivers. It may take a while to get used to and enjoy a new and different way of being with the child. A foster carer in a training workshop described how liberating it felt to tip out all the toys in the box, letting the child see all the toys and choose. Having the company of a clinician, or another interested adult, can encourage caregivers to establish a Watch Me Play! routine. Although the idea of slowing down and taking a step back seems appealing in principle to many caregivers, it also involves a change in tempo. Underlying anxieties about what children might show in their play, which could contribute to a reluctance to let children express themselves in their play, may need to be sensitively explored. As the examples in chapter 6 illustrate, for some carers the challenge is to wait to see what the child chooses to do, while for others it may be seeing the child using toys in a way that is different from what they expect.

Advocating for the psychological needs of babies and young children who have experienced adversity can require practitioners to take up a proactive role—for example, by sustaining multi-agency liaison and convening professional networks. The team around the child can then provide a forum in which direct observations can help to inform care planning and the preparation for transitions. Reflecting together about powerful feelings that may be conveyed by children's play, or that get in the way of allowing the child to play freely, can help to bring containment for those whose are closest to the child. Validating the contributions of all the adults who see the child, by showing interest in their observations and discussing them, provides protection against the potential impact of secondary trauma. This can help to mitigate painful dynamics that can leave professionals and family members alike feeling isolated and hopeless.

Clinicians themselves can gain much from the opportunity to carry out observational therapeutic work. Whether they are short or longer term, observational interventions provide a unique form of further professional development for clinicians, through experiential learning about the lives of young children in care and the complex dilemmas daily confronting foster carers and social workers.

Respectful relationships with caregivers and with children are the basis for facilitating collaborative working relationship as co-observers in Watch Me Play! Respect for the child's experiences involves the recognition that every child is unique and that the way things unfold is different for each child. Acknowledging that there are no quick solutions may be reassuring for foster carers when there are anxieties about whether the complexity of a child's needs and the demands of looking after the child can really be understood by those who are less closely involved. An interest in coming together to talk about what people see when a child is playing can be the first stage in creating an environment in which free play can flourish—a team around the child that is focused around the child's communications, experiences, and needs. Carers are more likely to be able to provide involved and attuned nurture for the children in their care when they are part of a culture that values their emotional commitment. Foster carers, special guardians, parents to whom a child has been returned, can pass on to their child the benefits of an ethos that values communication, development, and meaning.

As children become confident, they may begin to communicate more clearly and may be able to concentrate for longer. As their play becomes more sustained, less fleeting, perhaps with more pretend play, caregivers in turn may become more confident about noticing and understanding their child's signals. Regular attention to the child's play may also help to give foster carers and other professionals a clearer idea of the child's interests, skills, as well as any worries that may be troubling him or her. When professionals are able to share observations and understanding, anxieties can be reduced and the quality and stability of placements may improve. Feedback from social workers has highlighted the value of sharing observations for a better understanding of the child and the child's needs, particularly when difficult care-planning decisions have to be made—for example about placement moves or sibling placements.

Integrating different aspects of a child's life allows professionals to provide more containment for the child. Validating positive changes over time as well as recognizing difficulties and worries helps to establish meaningful relationships among professionals. Meetings of the network or the team around the child can become therapeutic in themselves when a state of wondering enters in, akin to a mother's reverie that allows her to contain her infant's uncertainties, fears, and distress. With the backing of an emotionally receptive network, a foster carer may feel more able to remain emotionally available to her foster child during transitions and times of difficulty.

# AFTERWORD

This book has described work in progress with babies and young children in care and their caregivers, using approaches based on attentive observation and reflection. Working alongside my colleagues in foster care, social work, health, and education, I have seen positive changes for children who have experienced trauma and disruption when they have been able to feel understood and held in mind by caregivers and responsible adults.

The stakes are high for children who have been maltreated by adults in their infancy and for those who have experienced repeated disruption of the most important factor for psychological well-being: a consistent and nurturing caregiver. Failure to address the impact of early trauma is costly to the individuals and families who are affected, and to society. Children whose cumulative adversities outweigh their natural resilience and zest for life suffer and struggle alone; some may seek a substitute for containment in criminal gangs or in substance abuse. I could have written a different book, about the catastrophic trajectories for children whose experiences of family conflict, mental illness, or violence are followed by repeated placement disruptions ultimately leading onto residential care. For some, the next stage is the criminal justice system and prison. For every child with a positive or more positive outcome, I know about many other children whose lives in the aftermath of maltreatment have remained overshadowed by severe, often transgenerational family distress; children who have experienced painful and repeated placement breakdowns; those who have been the subject of bitter disagreements among professionals; and those who have grown up never having been able to trust in or enjoy a stable relationship with a reliable adult.

Instead, I have selected examples and vignettes to bear witness to children's receptivity to adult attention, their eloquence if someone is watching and listening, and the support that an emotionally sensitive professional network can provide to help caregivers to go on reaching out to the vulnerable children in their care. I hope that parents and kinship carers, foster carers, and children's professionals may be encouraged to explore the power of attentive observation for themselves, and to seek out other parents and professionals with whom to share their observations and reflections.

## Attention

When we talk about attention in our culture, it is often in negative terms. Behaviour can be described as "attention-seeking", as if this were a criticism rather than a celebration of a child's natural seeking of acknowledgment and validation from the adults around the child, as natural and necessary as a plant turning towards the light of the sun.

Attention has a fundamental role in allowing a child to feel held in mind and to develop over time the internal continuity that sustains the personality and protects against the fragmenting impact of trauma: neuroscience provides the scientific evidence for connections in the brain that are generated during mutually rewarding interactions between caregivers and children. Sigmund Freud had a great deal to say about the power of attention as a life force and a form of psychic energy that gathers and binds perceptions together (1905e, 1950 [1895]; see also Stewart, 2013). Freud describes attention as a form of "observing thought" that looks for patterns of meaning and brings the ego—the conscious mind—into contact with reality (Freud, 1917d; see also Nagera, 2014).

Freud also saw attention as consisting of two aspects, one active, one more passive and receptive. The active aspect of attention "meets the sense-impressions half-way, instead of awaiting their appearance" (1911b, p. 220), while the more passive aspect of attention can be seen in the stance of evenly suspended attention that he recommends to psychoanalysts. This free-floating attention, receiving rather than selecting, allows the analyst the most direct contact with instinctual life (1912e, 1923a). In psychoanalytic observation, these aspects of attention are separated in time: the regular visit and the circumscribed role of the observer create a setting in which perceptions, both the conscious and the unconscious, can be taken in. The active aspect of attention, the observing thought that asks "What does this mean?", comes into play later, in the discussion in supervision and the continuing processing and reflection in the clinician's mind that this way of working facilitates. The reflective coming together of a professional network encompasses the coming together of caregiver and child and the coming together of thoughts and feelings that makes meaning, akin to the maternal reverie that Bion (1962) describes as fundamental to containment.

The energizing aspect of attention can be particularly helpful for those working and living with profoundly deprived children. A focus on learning together and on learning from experience can help to facilitate working alliances and to regulate the emotional labour of holding in mind the distress of the most vulnerable infants and young children. Whereas the dynamics of trauma are dominated by the compulsion to repeat, a group that is gathered together by attention has the potential to give birth to something new and lively.

# GLOSSARY

## Care proceedings and care orders

Under the Children Act 1989, a local authority can apply to the family courts for a **Care Order** if it believes a child is suffering or at risk of suffering significant harm.

Under **Section 20** of the Children Act, a child is voluntarily accommodated: a local authority provides care for children with the agreement of their parents, who continue to have parental responsibility.

An **Emergency Protection Order** can be granted for up to eight days to protect a child from significant harm.

An **Interim Care Order** may be granted at the start of care proceedings, lasting up to eight weeks and renewable for periods of up to four weeks.

If a **Full Care Order** is granted at the end of care proceedings, the local authority can place the child in long-term foster care.

A local authority can also apply for a **Placement Order** if they believe that the child should be adopted; or for a **Special Guardianship Order** under which a court appoints a carer—usually a relative—as the "Special Guardian" of a child until the child is 18.

*Professionals working with a child in care*

The group of professionals supporting a child in care is known as the **professional network**, or the **team around the child**.

**Foster carers** in the UK were known as foster parents until the 1990s.

They may be employed by a local authority or by an independent fostering agency. Foster carers are managed and supported by **Supervising Social Workers** (sometimes known as **Link Workers**).

A child in care has an allocated **Social Worker** who visits the child at least every six weeks.

An **Independent Reviewing Officer** chairs a **Looked-After Child Review** within twenty days of the child becoming looked after and every six months while the child remains in care.

Every child entering care has an **Initial Health Assessment**, usually by a community paediatrician, and a **Review Health Assessment** by a looked-after children's nurse, every six months for a child under five years, and every year for a child aged five years and over.

A child who is being placed for adoption or special guardianship has an **Adoption Medical,** which brings together the child's medical and developmental history.

In primary and secondary schools, a **Designated Teacher** has responsibility for coordinating support for children who are in care or have previously been in care. Each child in care has a **Personal Education Plan,** which is reviewed each school term.

# FURTHER READING AND RESOURCES

## On parenting and attachment

Daws, D., & de Rementeria, A. *Finding Your Way with Your Baby. The Emotional Life of Parents and Babies*. London: Routledge, 2015.

Gerhardt, S. *Why Love Matters. How Affection Shapes a Baby's Brain* (2nd edition). London: Routledge, 2015.

Murray, L., & Andrews, L. *The Social Baby: Understanding Babies' Communication from Birth*. Richmond, VA: The Children's Project/CP Publishing, 2005.

Prior, V., & Glaser, D. *Understanding Attachment and Attachment Disorders: Theory, Evidence and Practice*. London: Jessica Kingsley, 2006.

## Infant observation

Fawcett, M., & Watson, D. L. *Learning through Child Observation*. London: Jessica Kingsley, 2016.

Hingley-Jones, H., Parkinson, C., & Allain, L. (Eds.). *Observation in Health and Social Care: Applications for Learning, Research and Practice with Children and Adults*. London: Jessica Kingsley, 2017.

Miller, L., Rustin, M. E., Rustin, M. J., & Shuttleworth, J. (Eds.). *Closely Observed Infants*. London: Duckworth, 1989.

Reid, S. *Developments in Infant Observation. The Tavistock Model*. London: Routledge, 1997.

Urwin, C., & Sternberg, J. (Eds.). *Emotional Lives: Infant Observation and Research*. London: Routledge, 2012.
Youell, B. "Observation in social work practice." In: M. Bower (Ed.), *Psychoanalytic Theory for Social Work Practice: Thinking under Fire* (pp. 49–60). London: Routledge, 2005.

## Useful websites

The Association of Child Psychotherapists: https://childpsychotherapy.org.uk
The Association for Infant Mental Health (UK): https://aimh.org.uk
The Centre for the Developing Child at Harvard University: http://developingchild.harvard.edu/resources/
Coram BAAF (British Association for Adoption and Fostering): https://corambaaf.org.uk
Infant Observation: The International Journal of Infant Observation and Its Applications, published by Taylor and Francis: www.tandfonline.com/loi/riob20
Films by James and Joyce Robertson: www.robertsonfilms.info
The Social Baby: www.socialbaby.com
The Tavistock and Portman NHS Foundation Trust and training centre: https://tavistockandportman.nhs.uk
Understanding Childhood: www.understandingchildhood.net
The University of East Anglia Secure Base model: www.uea.ac.uk/providingasecurebase/resources
Zero to Three: https://www.zerotothree.org

# REFERENCES

Ainsworth, M. D. S., Blehar, M. C., Waters, E., & Wall, S. (1978). *Patterns of Attachment: A Psychological Study of the Strange Situation*. Hillsdale, NJ: Erlbaum.

APPG. (2015). *Building Great Britons. Conception to Age 2. The First 1001 Days*. London: All Party Parliamentary Group. Available at: https://plct.files.wordpress.com/2012/11/building-great-britons-report-conception-to-age-2-feb-2015.pdf

Allen, G. (2011). *Early Intervention: The Next Steps. An Independent Report to Her Majesty's Government*. London: Cabinet Office.

Alvarez, A. (2000). Discussion (II). In: J. Sandler, A.-M. Sandler, & R. Davies (Eds.), *Clinical and Observational Psychoanalytic Research: Roots of a Controversy* (pp. 100–107). London: Karnac.

American Academy of Pediatrics (2012). Neonatal drug withdrawal. *Pediatrics, 101* (6): e540–e560.

Anderson, J. (2006). Well-suited partners: Psychoanalytic research and grounded theory. *Journal of Child Psychotherapy, 32* (3): 329–348.

Association of Child Psychotherapists (2018). *Silent Catastrophe. Responding to the Danger Signs of Children and Young People's Mental Health Services in Trouble*. A Report from the Association of Child Psychotherapists on a Survey and Case Studies about NHS Child and Adolescent Mental Health Services. Available at: https://childpsychotherapy.org.uk/sites/

default/files/documents/ACP/20SILENT/20CATASTROPHE/20REPORT.pdf

Ayling, A., & Stringer, B. (2013). Supporting carer-child relationships through play: A model for teaching carers how to use play skills to strengthen attachment relationships. *Adoption and Fostering, 37* (2): 130–143.

Bardyshevsky, M. (1998). The compensation of autistic features during a little boy's second year: Overcoming pain through the development of attachment. *Infant Observation, 2* (1): 40–57.

Barlow, J., & Svanberg, P. O. (Eds.) (2009). *Keeping the Baby in Mind: Infant Mental Health in Practice.* London: Routledge.

Beckett, C., & McKeigue, B. (2003). Children in Limbo: Cases where court decisions have taken two years or more. *Adoption and Fostering, 27* (3): 31–40.

Beek, M., Neil, E., & Schofield, G. (2018). *Moving to Adoption: Research Review.* Norwich: Centre for Research on Children and Families, University of East Anglia.

Bentovim, A. (1992). *Trauma-Organized Systems.* London: Karnac.

Berridge, D. (1997). *Foster Care: A Research Review.* Norwich: Department of Health/The Stationery Office.

Berta, L., & Torchia, A. (1998). The contribution of infant observation to paediatrics. *Infant Observation, 2* (1): 79–89.

Bick, E. (1964). Notes on infant observation in psychoanalytic training. *International Journal of Psychoanalysis, 45*: 558–566.

Bick, E. (1968). The experience of the skin in early object relations. *International Journal of Psychoanalysis, 49*: 484.

Bion, W. R. (1961). *Experiences in Groups.* London: Tavistock.

Bion, W. R. (1962). A theory of thinking. *International Journal of Psychoanalysis, 43*: 306–310. Reprinted in: *Second Thoughts: Selected Papers on Psycho-Analysis* (pp. 110–119). London: Heinemann, 1967.

Bion, W. R. (1970). *Attention and Interpretation a Scientific Approach to Insight in Psycho-Analysis and Groups.* New York: Basic Books.

Blessing, D., & Block, K. (2014). Sewing on a shadow: Acquiring dimensionality in a participant observation. In: S. M. G. Adamo & M. E. Rustin (Eds.), *Young Child Observation: A Development in the Theory and Method of Infant Observation.* London: Karnac.

Bloom, S. L. (2003). Caring for the caregiver: Avoiding and treating vicarious traumatization. In: A. Giardino, E. Datner, & J. Asher (Eds.), *Sexual Assault, Victimization across the Lifespan* (pp. 459–470). Maryland Heights, MO: GW Medical Publishing. Available at: www.researchgate.net/publication/242223206_Caring_for_the_Caregiver_Avoiding_and_Treating_Vicarious_Trauma

Boswell, S., & Cudmore, L. (2014). "The children were fine": Acknowledging complex feelings in the move from foster care into adoption. *Fostering, 38* (1): 5–21.

Bower, M. (Ed.) (2005). *Psychoanalytic Theory for Social Work Practice. Thinking Under Fire.* London: Routledge.

Bowlby, J. (1969). *Attachment and Loss, Vol. 1: Attachment.* New York: Basic Books.

Brandon, M., Glaser, D., Maguire, S., McCrory, E., Lusney, C., & Ward, H. (2014). *Missed Opportunities: Indicators of Neglect—What Is Ignored, Why, and What Can Be Done? Research Report.* London: Department for Education/Childhood Wellbeing Research Centre. Available at: www.cwrc.ac.uk/documents/RR404_Indicators_of_neglect_missed_op portunities.pdf

Bridge, G., & Miles, G. (1996). *On the Outside Looking In.* London: Central Council for Education and Training in Social Work.

Briskman, J., & Scott, S. (2012). *Randomised Controlled Trial of the Fostering Changes Programme, The National Academy for Parenting Research.* Report for the Department for Education. London: King's College London.

Britton, R. (1983). Breakdown and reconstitution of the family circle. In: M. Boston & R. Szur (Eds.), *Psychotherapy with Severely Disturbed Children* (pp. 105–109). London: Routledge & Kegan Paul.

Browning, A. S. (2015). Undertaking planned transitions for children in out-of-home care. *Adoption and Fostering, 39* (1): 51–61.

Bruner, J. (1983). *Child's Talk. Learning to Use Language.* Oxford: Oxford University Press.

Callaghan, J., Young, B., Pace, F., & Vostanis, P. (2004). Evaluation of a new mental health service for looked-after children. *Clinical Child Psychology and Psychiatry, 9* (1): 130–148.

Cardenal, M. (1999). A psychoanalytically informed approach to clinically ill babies. *Infant Observation, 2* (1): 90–101.

Clyman, R. B., & Harden, B. J. (2002). Infants in foster and kinship care. *Infant Mental Health Journal, 23* (5): 435–453.

Craven, P. A., & Lee, R. (2006). Therapeutic interventions for foster children. A systematic research synthesis. *Research on Social Work Practice, 16* (3): 287–304.

Cregeen, S. (2017). A place within the heart: Finding a home with parental objects. *Journal of Child Psychotherapy, 43* (2): 159–174.

Daws, D. (1999). Child psychotherapy in general practice. *Clinical Child Psychology and Psychiatry, 4* (1): 1359.

Daws, D., & de Rementeria, A. (2015). *Finding Your Way with Your Baby. The Emotional Life of Parents and Babies.* London: Routledge.

Delion, P. (2000). The application of Esther Bick's method to the observation of babies at risk of autism. *Infant Observation, 3* (3): 84–90.

DfE (2017). *Children Looked After in England (Including Adoption), Year Ending 31 March 2017. SFR 50/2017. National Statistics.* London: Department for Education. Available at: https://assets.publishing.service.gov.uk/gov ernment/uploads/system/uploads/attachment_data/file/664995/ SFR50_2017-Children_looked_after_in_England.pdf

Dimigen, G., Del Priore, C., & Butler, S. (1999). Psychiatric disorder among children at time of entering local authority care: Questionnaire survey. *British Medical Journal, 319*: 675.

Dozier, M., & Lindhiem, O. (2006). This is my child: Differences among foster parents in commitment to their young children. *Child Maltreatment, 11*: 338–345.

Dozier, M., Lindhiem, O., Lewis, E., Bick, J., Bernard, K., & Peloso, E. (2009). Effects of a Foster Parent training on young children's attachment behaviors: Preliminary evidence from a randomized clinical trial. *Child and Adolescent Social Work, 26*: 321–332.

Dugnat, M. (2001). *Observer un bébé avec attention?* Paris: Eres.

Dugnat, M., & Arama, M. (2001). Introduction. Pour une observation tempérée au service de l'attention et de la prévention. In: M. Dugnat (Ed.), *Observer un bébé avec attention?* (pp. 11–26). Paris: Eres.

Elliot, A. J., & Reis, H. T. (2003). Attachment and exploration in adulthood. *Journal of Personality and Social Psychology, 85* (2): 317–331.

Emanuel, L. (2006). The contribution of organisational dynamics to the triple deprivation of looked-after children. In: J. Kenrick, C. Lindsey, & L. Tollemache (Eds.), *Creating New Families: Therapeutic Approaches to Fostering, Adoption and Kinship Care* (pp. 163–179). London: Karnac.

Fahlberg, V. (1991). *A Child's Journey Through Placement.* Indianapolis, IN: Perspective Press, 2012.

Family Rights Group (2018). *The Care Crisis Review: Options for Change.* London: Author.

Farmer, E., & Lutman, E. (2010). *Case Management and Outcomes for Neglected Children Returned to Their Parents. A Five Year Follow-Up Study.* Bristol: University of Bristol; London: Department for Education.

Fawcett, M., & Watson, D. L. (2016). *Learning through Child Observation.* London: Jessica Kingsley.

Ferguson, H. (2017). How children become invisible in child protection work: Findings from research into day-to-day social work practice. *British Journal of Social Work, 47* (4): 1007–1023.

Fletcher, A. (1983). Working in a Neonatal Intensive Care Unit. *Journal of Child Psychotherapy, 9* (1): 47–56.

Fraiberg, S. (1982). Pathological defenses in infancy. *Psychoanalytic Quarterly*, 51: 612–635.

Freud, A., & Burlingham, D. (1944). Reports on the Hampstead Nurseries. In: *Infants without Families, and Reports on the Hampstead Nurseries 1939–1945*. London: Hogarth Press.

Freud, S. (1905e). *Jokes and Their Relation to the Unconscious. Standard Edition 8*.

Freud, S. (1911b). Formulations on the two principles of mental functioning. *Standard Edition, 12*.

Freud, S. (1912e). Recommendations to physicians practising psycho-analysis. *Standard Edition 12*.

Freud, S. (1917d). A metapsychological supplement to the theory of dreams. *Standard Edition 14*.

Freud, S. (1923a). Two encyclopaedia articles. *Standard Edition 18*.

Freud, S. (1950 [1895]). Project for a scientific psychology. *Standard Edition 1*.

Geraldini, S. A. R. (2016). Becoming a person: Learning from observing premature babies and their mothers. *Infant Observation, 19* (1): 42–59.

Gerhardt, S. (2015). *Why Love Matters: How Affection Shapes a Baby's Brain* (2nd edition). London: Routledge.

Gerin, E. I., Hanson, E., Viding, E., & McCrory, E. J. (2019). A review of childhood maltreatment, latent vulnerability and the brain: Implications for clinical practice and prevention. *Adoption & Fostering* (in press).

Gilbert, R., Spatz Widom, C., Browne, K., Ferguson, D., Webb, E., & Janson, S. (2009). Child maltreatment series 1: Burden and consequences of child maltreatment in high-income countries. *Lancet, 373*: 68–81.

Glaser, B., & Strauss, A. L. (1967). *The Discovery of Grounded Theory: Strategies for Qualitative Research*. New Brunswick, NJ: Aldine.

Grossman, K. E., Grossman, K., & Waters, E. (2005). Early care and the roots of attachment and partnership representations: The Bielefeld and Regensburg longitudinal studies. In: K. E. Grossman, K. Grossman, & E. Waters (Eds.), *Attachment from Infancy to Adulthood* (pp. 98–136). New York: Guilford Press.

Haag, M. (2002). *A propos et à partir de l'oeuvre et de la personne d'Esther Bick, Vol. 1. La méthode d'Esther Bick pour l'observation régulière et prolongée du tout petit au sein de sa famille*. Paris: Livres Autoedition.

Hall, J. (2009). Work in progress: Developing a flexible model of therapeutic observation of young mothers and their infants in care proceedings. *Infant Observation, 12* (3): 358–364.

Halton, W. (1994). Some unconscious aspects of organizational life. In: A. Obholzer & V. Z. Roberts (Eds.), *The Unconscious at Work: Individual and Organizational Stress in the Human Services* (pp. 11–18). London: Routledge.

Halton, W. (2014). Obsessional-punitive defences in care systems: Menzies Lyth revisited. In: D. Armstrong (Ed.), *Social Defences Against Anxiety: Explorations in a Paradigm* (pp. 27–38). London: Routledge.

Hardy, C., Hackett, E., Murphy, E., Cooper, B., Ford, T., & Conroy, S. (2013). Mental health screening and early intervention: Clinical research study for under 5-year-old children in care in an inner London borough. *Clinical Child Psychology and Psychiatry, 20*: 261–275.

Harvard Center for the Developing Child (2018). *Serve and Return Interaction.* Available at: https://developingchild.harvard.edu/science/key-concepts/serve-and-return/Website

Hillen, T., Gafson, L., Drage, L., & Conlan, L. M. (2012). Assessing the prevalence of mental health disorders and needs among preschool children in care in England. *Infant Mental Health Journal, 33* (4): 411–420.

Hindle, D. (2007). Clinical research: A psychotherapeutic assessment model for siblings in care. *Journal of Child Psychotherapy, 33* (1): 70–93.

Hindle, D. (Ed.) (2008). *The Emotional Experience of Adoption: A Psychoanalytic Perspective.* London: Routledge.

Hingley-Jones, H. (2017). From observation, via reflection, to practice: Psychoanalytic baby and young child observation and the helping professions. In: H. Hingley-Jones, C. Parkinson, & L. Allain (Eds.), *Observation in Health and Social Care: Applications for Learning, Research and Practice with Children and Adults* (pp. 21–39). London: Jessica Kingsley.

Holton, J. A. (2007). The coding process and its challenges. In: A. Bryant & K. Charmaz (Eds.), *The Sage Handbook of Grounded Theory* (pp. 265–281). London: Sage.

Houzel, D. (1996). The family envelope and what happens when it is torn. *International Journal of Psychoanalysis, 77* (5): 901–912.

Houzel, D. (1999). A therapeutic application of infant observation in child psychiatry. *Infant Observation, 2* (3): 42–53.

Houzel, D. (2008). Les applications préventives et thérapeutiques de la méthode d'Esther Bick. In: P. Delion (Ed.), *L'observation du bébé selon Esther Bick. Son intérêt dans la pédopsychiatrie aujourd'hui* (pp. 81–94). Paris: Eres.

Howe, D. (2005). *Child Abuse and Neglect: Attachment, Development and Intervention.* London: Palgrave.

Hoxter, S. (1977). Play and communication. In: M. Boston & D. Daws (Eds.), *The Child Psychotherapist and Problems of Young People* (pp. 202–231). London: Wildwood House.

Humphreys, C., & Kiraly, M. (2011). High-frequency family contact: A road to nowhere for infants. *Child and Family Social Work, 16*: 1–11.

Kenrick, J. (2009). Concurrent planning 1. A retrospective study of the continuities and discontinuities of care, and their impact on the development of infants and young children placed for adoption by the Coram Concurrent Planning Project. *Adoption and Fostering, 33* (4): 5–18.

Kenrick, J. (2010). Concurrent planning 2: The roller-coaster of uncertainty. *Adoption and Fostering, 34* (2): 38–47.

Kenrick, J., Lindsey, C., & Tollemache, L. (2006). *Creating New Families: Therapeutic Approaches to Fostering, Adoption and Kinship Care.* London: Karnac.

Klee, L., Kronstadt, D., & Zlotnick, C. (1997). Foster care's youngest: A preliminary report. *American Journal of Orthopsychiatry, 6* (2): 290–299.

Klein, M. (1958). *On the Development of Mental Functioning: Envy and Gratitude and Other Works, 1946–1963. The Writings of Melanie Klein, Volume III.* London: Hogarth Press, 1975.

Lanyado, M. (2003). The emotional tasks of moving from fostering to adoption: Transitions, attachment, separation and loss. *Clinical Child Psychiatry and Psychology, 8* (3): 337–349.

Lazar, R. A., & Ermann, G. (1998). Learning to be: The observation of a premature baby. *Infant Observation, 2* (1): 21–39.

Le Riche, P., & Tanner, K. (Eds.) (1998). *Observation and Its Application to Social Work: Rather Like Breathing.* London: Jessica Kingsley.

Lechevalier, B., Fellouse, J.-C., & Bonnesoeur, S. (2000). West's syndrome and infantile autism: The effect of a psychotherapeutic approach in certain cases. *Infant Observation, 3* (3): 23–38.

Lieberman, A. F. (2002). Ambiguous outcomes, imperfect tools: Challenges on interaction with young children in foster care and their families. *Bulletin of Zero to Three, 22* (5): 4–8.

Lobatto, W. (2016). Working with professional systems. In: S. Barratt & W. Lobatto (Eds.), *Surviving and Thriving in Care and Beyond: Personal and Professional Perspectives.* London: Karnac.

Maiello, S. (1997). Twinning phantasies in the mother-infant couple and the observer's counterpoint function: Preliminary remarks about the numbers one, two and three. *Infant Observation, 1* (1): 31–50.

Maiello, S. (2007). Containment and differentiation: Notes on the observer's maternal and paternal function. *Infant Observation, 10* (1): 41–49.

Main, M., & Solomon, J. (1980). Procedures for identifying infants as disorganized/disoriented during the Ainsworth strange situation. In: M. T. Greenberg, D. Cicchetti, & E. M. Cummings (Eds.), *Attachment in the Preschool Years* (pp. 161–185). Chicago, IL: University of Chicago Press.

Masson, J. (2016). Reforming care proceedings in England and Wales: Speeding up justice and welfare? In: J. Eekelaar (Ed.), *Family Law in Britain and America in the New Century: Essays in Honor of Sanford N. Katz* (pp. 187–206). Leiden: Brill.

Masson, J., Dickens, J., Bader, K., Garside, L., & Young, J. (2017). Achieving positive change for children? Reducing the length of child protection proceedings: Lessons from England and Wales. *Adoption and Fostering, 41*: 401–413.

McAuley, C., & Young, C. (2006). The mental health needs of looked after children: Challenges for CAMHs provision. *Journal of Social Work Practice, 20* (1): 91–104.

McCann, J., James, A., Wilson, S., & Dunn, G. (1996). Prevalence of psychiatric disorders in young people in the care system. *British Medical Journal, 313* (15): 29–30.

McCrory, E., De Brito, S., & Viding, E. (2011). Heightened neural reactivity to threat in child victims of family violence. *Current Biology, 21* (23): R947–R948.

McFadyen, A. (1994). *Special Care Babies and Their Developing Relationships.* London: Routledge.

Meakings, S., & Selwyn, J. (2016). "She was a foster mother who said she didn't give cuddles": The adverse early foster care experiences of children who later struggle with adoptive family life. *Clinical Child Psychology and Psychiatry, 21* (4): 509–519.

Meins, E., & Fernyhough, C. (2010). *Mind-Mindedness Coding Manual, Version 2.0.* Unpublished manuscript. Durham, UK: Durham University.

Meins, E., Fernyhough, C., Wainwright, R., Clark-Carter, D., Das Gupta, M., Fradley, E., & Tuckey, M. (2003). Pathways to understanding mind: Construct validity and predictive validity of maternal mind-mindedness. *Child Development, 74*: 1194–1211.

Meltzer, H., Corbin, T., Gatward, R., Goodman, R., & Ford, T. (2003). *The Mental Health of Young People Looked After by Local Authorities in England.* London: The Stationery Office.

Mendelsohn, A. (2005). Recovering reverie: Using infant observation in interventions with traumatised mothers and their premature babies. *Infant Observation, 8* (3): 195–205.

Milford, R., Kleve, L., Lea, J., & Greenwqood, R. (2006). A pilot evaluation study of the Solihull Approach. *Community Practitioner, 79* (11): 358–362.

Miller, L., Rustin, M. E., Rustin, M. J., & Shuttleworth, J. (Eds.) (1989). *Closely Observed Infants.* London: Duckworth.

Muir, E. (1992). Watching, waiting, and wondering: Applying psychoanalytic principles to mother-infant interaction. *Infant Mental Health Journal, 13*: 319–328.

Murray, L., & Andrews, L. (2005). *The Social Baby: Understanding Babies' Communication from Birth.* Richmond, VA: The Children's Project/CP Publishing.

Music, G. (2016). *Nurturing Natures: Attachment and Children's Emotional, Social and Brain Development.* Abingdon: Routledge.

Nagera, H. (Ed.) (2014). *Basic Psychoanalytic Concepts on Metapsychology, Conflicts, Anxiety and Other Subjects.* London: Routledge.

Narey, M., & Oates, M. (2018). *Foster Care in England: A Review for the Department for Education.* London: Department for Education. Available at: https://assets.publishing.service.gov.uk/government/uploads/system/uploads/attachment_data/file/679320/Foster_Care_in_England_Review.pdf

National Adoption Leadership Board (2014). *Impact of Court Judgments on Adoption: What the Judgments Do and Do Not Say.* Available at: https://www.first4adoption.org.uk/wp-content/uploads/2014/11/ALB-Impact-of-Court-Judgments-on-Adoption-November-2014.pdf

Negri, R. (1994). *The Newborn in the Intensive Care Unit: A Neuropsychoanalytic Prevention Model* (Revised edition). London: Karnac, 2014.

Neil, E., & Howe, D. (2004). *Contact in Adoption and Permanent Foster Care: Research, Theory and Practice.* London: BAAF.

NICE/SCIE (2010). *Public Health Guidance: Promoting the Quality of Life of Looked-After Children and Young People.* Public Health Guideline 28. London: National Institute for Clinical Excellence. Available at: www.nice.org.uk/guidance/ph28

Nutt, L. (2006). *The Lives of Foster Carers: Private Sacrifices, Public Restrictions.* London: Routledge.

Onions, C. (2018). Retaining foster carers during challenging times: The benefits of embedding reflective practice into the foster carer role. *Adoption and Fostering, 42* (3): 249–256.

Pallet, C., Blackeby, K., Yule, W., Weissman, R., & Scott, S. (2000). *Fostering Changes: How to Improve Relationships and Manage Difficult Behaviour. A Training Programme for Foster Carers.* London: BAAF.

Panksepp, J. (2007). Can play diminish ADHD and facilitate the construction of the social brain? *Journal of the Canadian Academy of Child and Adolescent Psychiatry, 16* (2): 57–66.

Parkinson, C., Allain, L., & Hingley-Jones, H. (2017). Introduction: Observation for our times. In: H. Hingley-Jones, C. Parkinson, & L. Allain (Eds.), *Observation in Health and Social Care: Applications for Learning, Research and Practice with Children and Adults* (pp. 9–18). London: Jessica Kingsley.

Perry, B. D., Pollard, R. A., Blakley, T. L., Baker, W. L., & Vigilante, D. (1995). Childhood trauma, the neurobiology of adaptation and "use dependent" development of the brain: How "states become traits". *Infant Mental Health Journal, 16*: 271–291.

Philps, J. (2003). *Applications of Child Psychotherapy to Work with Children in Temporary Foster Care*. Doctoral dissertation, Tavistock Centre/University of East London, London.

Prior, V., & Glaser, D. (2006). *Understanding Attachment and Attachment Disorders: Theory, Evidence, and Practice*. London: Jessica Kingsley.

Reams, R. (1999). Children birth to three entering the state's custody. *Infant Mental Health Journal, 20* (2): 166–174.

Reddy, V., & Mireault, G. (2015). Teasing and clowning in infancy. *Current Biology, 25* (1): 20–23.

Reid, S. (Ed.) (1997). *Developments in Infant Observation: The Tavistock Model*. London: Routledge.

Rhode, M. (2007). Infant observation as an early intervention. In: S. Acquarone (Ed.), *Signs of Autism in Infants: Recognition and Early Intervention* (pp. 193–211). London: Karnac.

Robertson, J., & Robertson, J. (1952). *A Two-Year Old Goes to the Hospital*. Available at: www.robertsonfilms.info/2_year_old.htm

Robertson, J., & Robertson, J. (1989). *Separation and the Very Young*. London: Free Association Books.

Ruch, G. (2017). Foreword. In: H. Hingley-Jones, C. Parkinson, & L. Allain (Eds.), *Observation in Health and Social Care: Applications for Learning, Research and Practice with Children and Adults* (pp. 77–78). London: Jessica Kingsley.

Rushton, A. (2007). *The Adoption of Looked After Children: A Scoping Review of Research*. London: Social Care Institute for Excellence/The Policy Press.

Rustin, M. E. (1999). Multiple families in mind. *Clinical Child Psychology and Psychiatry, 4* (1): 51–62.

Rustin, M. E. (2005). A conceptual analysis of critical moments in Victoria Climbié's life. *Child and Family Social Work, 10* (1): 11–19.

Rustin, M. E. (2009). Esther Bick's legacy of infant observation at the Tavistock: Some reflections 60 years on. *Infant Observation, 12* (1): 29–41.

Rustin, M. E. (2014). The relevance of infant observation for early intervention: Containment in theory and practice. *Infant Observation, 17* (2): 97–114.

Rustin, M. E. (2018). Creative responses to compromised beginnings in life: How to support families struggling with early difficulties. *Infant Observation, 20* (2–3): 148–160.

Rustin, M. E. & Rustin, M. J. (2019). *New Discoveries in Child Psychotherapy: Findings from Qualitative Research*. London: Routledge.

Rustin, M. J. (2001). Research, evidence and psychotherapy. In: C. Mace, S. Moorey, & B. Roberts (Eds.), *Evidence in the Psychological Therapies: A Critical Guide for Practitioners* (pp. 27–45). London: Brunner-Routledge.

Rustin, M. J. (2012). Infant observation as a method of research. In: C. Urwin & J. Sternberg (Eds.), *Infant Observation and Research: Emotional Processes in Everyday Lives* (pp. 13–22). London: Routledge.

Rutter, M. (1998). Developmental catch up and deficit following adoption after severe global early privation. The English and Romanian Adoptees ERS study team. *Journal of Child Psychology and Psychiatry, 39*: 465–476.

Rutter, M. (2003). Genetic influences on risk and protection: Implications for understanding resilience. In: S. Luthar (Ed.), *Resilience and Vulnerability: Adaptation in the Context of Childhood Adversities.* Cambridge: Cambridge University Press.

Schein, S., Roben, C., Costello, A., & Dozier, M. (2017). Implementing attachment and biobehavioural catch-up with foster parents. *International Journal of Birth and Parent Education, 5* (2): 22–26.

Schofield, G., & Beek, M. (2018). *Secure Base Model: Introductory Talk.* Norwich: Center for Research on Children and Families, University of East Anglia. Available at: www.uea.ac.uk/providingasecurebase/resources

Schore, A. (2001). The effects of early relational trauma on right brain development, affect regulation and infant mental health. *Infant Mental Health Journal, 22* (1–2): 201–269.

Selwyn, J., Harris, P., Quinton, D., Nawaz, S., Wijedasa, D., & Wood, M. (2008). *Pathways to Permanence for Black, Asian and Mixed Ethnicity Children.* London: BAAF/Adoption Research Initiative.

Selwyn, J., Magnus, L., & Stuijfzand, B. (2018). *Our Lives Our Care. Looked After Children's Views on Their Well-Being in 2017.* Bristol: University of Bristol School for Policy Studies and Coram Voice. Available at: www. researchgate.net/publication/323345369_Selwyn_Jet_al2018_Our_Li fe_Our_Care_looked_after_childrens_views_on_their_well-being_in_2017_full_report

Selwyn, J., Wijedasa, D., & Meakings, S. (2014). *Beyond the Adoption Order: Challenges, Interventions and Adoption Disruption. Research Report.* London: Department for Education.

Sinclair, I., Gibbs, I., & Wilson, W. (2004). *Foster Carers: Why They Stay and Why They Leave.* London: Jessica Kingsley.

Slade, A. (1994). Making meaning and making believe: Their role in the clinical process. In A. Slade & D. Wolf (Eds.), *Children at Play: Clinical and Developmental Approaches to Meaning and Representation* (pp. 81–107). New York: Oxford University Press.

Solihull Approach (2018). *Understanding Your Child's Behaviour.* Available at: http://solihullapproachparenting.com/wp-content/uploads/delightful-downloads/2016/06/Lets-Play-Updated.pdf

Spitz, R. A. (1945). Hospitalism: An inquiry into the genesis of psychiatric conditions in early childhood. *Psychoanalytic Study of the Child, 1*: 53–74.

Stahmer, A. C., Leslie, L. K., Hurlburt, M., Barth, R. P., Webb, M. B., Landsverk, J., & Zhang, J. (2005). Developmental and behavioral needs and service use for young children in child welfare. *Pediatrics, 116*: 891–900.

Steiner, J. (1985). Turning a blind eye: The cover up for Oedipus. *International Review of Psycho-Analysis, 12*: 161–172.

Steiner, J. (1993). *Psychic Retreats: Pathological Organisations in Psychotic, Neurotic and Borderline Patients*. London: Routledge.

Stern, D. N. (2004). *The First Relationship: Infant and Mother*. Cambridge, MA: Harvard University Press.

Sternberg, J. (2005). *Infant Observation at the Heart of Training*. London: Karnac.

Stewart, W. A. (2013). *Psychoanalysis: The First Ten Years 1888–1898*. London: Routledge.

Sunderland, M. (2007). *What Every Parent Needs to Know: The Incredible Effects of Love, Nurture and Play on Your Child's Development*. London: Dorling Kindersley.

Tanner, K. (1999). Observation: A counter culture offensive: Observation's contribution to the development of reflective social work practice. *Infant Observation, 2* (2): 12–32.

Tarsoly, E. (1998). The relationship between failures in containment and early feeding difficulties: A participant observational study in a Hungarian residential nursery. *Infant Observation, 2* (1): 58–78.

Tiltina, K. (2015). *Challenges Facing Long-Term Foster Carers: An Exploration of the Nature of Psychoanalytic Parent/Carer Support*. Child Professional Doctorate thesis, Tavistock and Portman NHS Foundation Trust, London.

Trevarthen, C. (2001). Intrinsic motives for companionship in understanding their origin, development, and significance for infant mental health. *Infant Mental Health Journal, 22* (1–2): 95–131.

Trowell, J., & Rustin, M. E. (1991). Developing the internal observer in professionals in training. *Infant Mental Health Journal, 12* (3): 233–246.

Tustin, F. (1986). *Autistic Barriers in Neurotic Patients*. London: Karnac.

Uglow, J. (1997). *Hogarth: A Life and a World*. London: Faber & Faber.

Ungar, T. (2017). Neuroscience, joy, and the well-infant visit that got me thinking. *Annals of Family Medicine, 15* (1): 80–83.

Urquiza, A. J., Wirtz, S. J., Peterson, M. S., & Singer, V. A. (1994). Screening and evaluating abused and neglected children entering protective custody. *Child Welfare, 73*: 155–171.

Urwin, C., & Sternberg, J. (2012). *Emotional Lives: Infant Observation and Research*. London: Routledge.

Vamos, J., Tardos, A., Golse, B., & Konicheckis, A. (2010). *Contribution of the Pikler Approach to What Is Known with Regard to a Baby's Resources*. Lecture at the 12th Congress of the World Association of Infant Mental Health, Leipzig, Germany.

Waddell, M. (2006). Infant observation in Britain: The Tavistock approach. *International Journal of Psychoanalysis, 87*: 1103–1120.

Wade, J., Biehal, N., Farrelly, N., & Sinclair, I. (2010). *Maltreated Children in the Looked-After System: A Comparison of Outcomes for Those Who Go Home and Those Who Do Not*. London: Department for Education. Available at: www.education.gov.uk/publications/eOrderingDownload/DFE-RBX-10-06.pdf

Wakelyn, J. (2011). Therapeutic observation of an infant in foster care. *Journal of Child Psychotherapy, 37* (3): 280–310.

Wakelyn, J. (2012a). Observation as a therapeutic intervention for infants and young children in care. *Infant Observation, 15* (1): 49–66.

Wakelyn, J. (2012b). A study of therapeutic observation of an infant in foster care. In: C. Urwin & J. Sternberg (Eds.), *Emotional Lives: Infant Observation and Research* (pp. 81–92). London: Routledge.

Wakelyn, J. (2018). *Evaluation of Watch Me Play! Training*. Unpublished research report. London: Tavistock Clinic Foundation.

Wakelyn, J. (2019). *Watch Me Play!: A Manual*. Available at: https://tavistockandportman.nhs.uk/care-and-treatment/our-clinical-services/first-step

Ward, H., Brown, R., Westlake, D., & Munro, E. R. (2010). *Infants Suffering, or Likely to Suffer, Significant Harm: A Prospective Longitudinal Study*. Research Brief, DFE-RB053. London: Department for Education.

Ward, H., Munro, E., & Dearden, C. (2006). *Babies and Young Children in Care: Life Pathways, Decision-Making and Practice*. London: Jessica Kingsley.

Watillon-Naveau, A. (2008). Behind the mirror: Interviews with parents whose baby has been observed according to Esther Bick's method. *Infant Observation, 11* (2): 215–223.

WHO (2004). *The Importance of Caregiver-Child Interactions for the Survival and Healthy Development of Young Children: A Review*. Geneva: World Health Organization. Available at: www.who.int/child-adolescent-health

Williams, G. (1998). Reflections on some particular dynamics of eating disorders. In: R. Anderson (Ed.), *Facing It Out: Clinical Perspectives on Adolescent Disturbance*. London: Duckworth.

Winnicott, D. W. (1951). Transitional objects and transitional phenomena. In: *Through Paediatrics to Psychoanalysis: Collected Papers* (pp. 229–242). London: Karnac, 1984.

Winnicott, D. W. (1962). Ego integration in child development. In: *The Maturational Processes and the Facilitating Environment* (pp. 56–63). London: Hogarth Press, 1965.

Winnicott, D. W. (1967). The concept of a healthy individual. In: *Home Is Where We Start From*. Harmondsworth: Penguin, 1986.

Wittenberg, I. (1999). What is psychoanalytic about the Tavistock model of studying infants? Does it contribute to psychoanalytic knowledge? *Infant Observation, 2* (3): 4–15.

Youell, B. (2005). Observation in social work practice. In: M. Bower (Ed.), *Psychoanalytic Theory for Social Work Practice: Thinking Under Fire*. London: Routledge.

# INDEX